Free to Leave,
Free to Stay

Free to Leave, Free to Stay

Fruits of the Spirit and Church Choice

JANA MARGUERITE BENNETT
and MELISSA MUSICK NUSSBAUM

CASCADE *Books* · Eugene, Oregon

FREE TO LEAVE, FREE TO STAY
Fruits of the Spirit and Church Choice

Cascade Books
A Division of Wipf and Stock Publishers
199 W. 8th Ave., Suite 3
Eugene, OR 97401

www.wipfandstock.com

ISBN 13: 978-1-55635-899-9

Cataloging-in-Publication data:

Bennett, Jana Marguerite.

Free to leave, free to stay : fruits of the spirit and church choice / Jana Marguerite Bennett and Melissa Musick Nussbaum.

    viii + 114 p. ; 23 cm. — Includes bibliographical references.

    ISBN 13: 978-1-55635-899-9

    1. Church Membership. 2. Faith Development. I. Nussbaum, Melissa Musick. II. Title.

BV601.7.F66 2008

Table of Contents

Devotional Interludes

Authors' Note

Paul begins his list of the fruits of the Holy Spirit with love and joy. He ends it with gentleness and self-control. We reversed the order in our book, as we did, quite unconsciously at the beginning, in our writing of the chapters. We intuited the need to consider the more modest gifts, such as self-control, first, because we came to understand their necessity to the whole. Just as most of us don't really long to be the toe on the Body of Christ, though toes are critical to a sound body, so most of us would prefer one of the more exalted gifts—love or joy—over the modest ones. But without the tended fields of self-control, say, or gentleness, there is no place for love to take root and grow. This re-ordering was helpful for us; we hope it will prove helpful to the reader.

The questions of leaving or staying in a community are questions of discernment. The devotional interludes between the chapters are not meant as an exhaustive look at the ways of listening to God and seeing the signs of God's leading. Rather, we chose this small sample from a variety of Christian traditions as an introduction to the riches of devotional and spiritual writing available to us. Discernment is not a path we have to walk alone. We have worthy companions for the journey.

Our scripture texts are taken from the New Revised Standard Version of the Holy Bible. In some of the conversion stories presented here, we use pseudonyms and change some details, either at the request of the storyteller or because more people are involved than we could ask permission. We are grateful for all the holy men and women, from our cradles onward, who taught us the Scriptures and sang us the Scriptures and so helped us to fall in love with its beauty and its truth.

Introduction

Melissa Musick Nussbaum

Christ led me into the monastery and Christ led me out of the monastery.
— John Zay

I was nearly twenty when I left the Methodist church of my childhood. My maternal great-grandfather was a circuit rider, one of the itinerant preachers who brought Methodism to Texas. I grew up less than a block from church, and I spent every Sunday there: first Sunday School, then the worship service, and then home for dinner. After dinner I was back for youth group and the evening service. Until I met my husband, I had never dated a boy outside my church.

In the summers, I went to visit my father's Southern Baptist family in the small town where I was born. I looked forward to the two-week Vacation Bible School and the nightly tent revivals. My favorite evangelist was an old blind man who preached a railroad sermon. The tracks on the road to hell, he thundered, were a wide gauge, but the tracks on the road to heaven were narrow, and not all our cars were going to make the journey. He stayed on the narrow way by never dancing. "I never needed a dance floor or a honky-tonk band to get my arms around my wife."

The tent filled with moths clustered around the strings of electric bulbs as he bade us, like the moths seeking the light, to come forward and be saved. I went down to the front as often as my grandmother would allow. One night, she grabbed my hand and pulled me back onto the metal folding chair. "You are saved," she hissed. "Now, sit down."

My mother told me years later that Ma-Maw was worried I would be stepped on or knocked over "by some drunk cowboy from Silverton" who, in his haste to get right with Jesus, wouldn't notice a small, kneeling child.

This is a part of my life my children never witnessed. They are Roman Catholics and they forget that I was ever not one as well. When my oldest daughter interned with the Frontier Nurses in Hyden, Kentucky, I went to visit her. She had grown close to a woman who worshiped every Sunday at the Hurt's Creek Church of Christ. Elisabeth warned me that the service would seem strange. She wanted me to be prepared for an unsettling experience. We went in. We opened our hymnals and began to sing. "Up from the grave he arose," I sang out, "with a mighty triumph o'er His foes."

Elisabeth looked at me, surprised. "You know this hymn?" she whispered.

"You could wake me from a dead sleep," I whispered back, "and I could sing all the verses."

My children know all the verses to "On Eagle's Wings," but I rocked them to sleep with "Softly and Tenderly," "Abide with Me," and "Standing on the Promises." I was glad to sing with the men and women of the Hurt's Creek Church of Christ. The music took me to my childhood home and reminded me of all that I miss the most of those days and that place.

I was still a child when I left home, and I left home in many ways, becoming the first Catholic on either side of my family for as far back as anyone can remember. Surely some of them thought I had switched onto to a dangerously wide-gauge track.

There was no anger in my leaving, and certainly little doctrinal consideration. I had, in the way of the young, fallen in love: with my husband and with the liturgy. I remember hearing the Eucharistic Prayer for the first time and thinking that I had always been walking towards these words. But I carry with me still the pang of leaving the ones who formed me in faith and who were, from my earliest days, the face of Christ ever before me.

As with any move, I could not bring everything with me to the new dwelling. The music of John and Charles Wesley has found its way into the American Catholic Church, but it has been years since I stood in church and sang Wesley's,

> O for a thousand tongues to sing
>
> My great redeemer's praise,
>
> The glories of my God and King,
>
> The triumphs of His grace!

Hear Him, ye deaf;

His praise, ye dumb,

Your loosed tongues employ;

Ye blind, behold your Savior come;

And leap, ye lame, for joy.

I've yet to meet a cradle Catholic who can sing all the books of the New Testament, in order, or who can recount the deaths of Ananias and Sapphira in song. Sing about Zaccheus as a small child, I tell them, and you will never forget his climb up and down the sycamore tree.

When Saint Benedict wrote his rule for religious life, he understood the costs of stability, but he was wise enough to know its benefits, as well. He knew the hard-won gift of learning to live with the same people in the same place, for life. The promise and problem of stability is the problem and promise of married life every bit as much as it is for monastic life. What are the problems and promises of stability in church life?

In his rule, Saint Benedict decrees that a man entering the monastic life "is to promise, before God and His Saints to be stable, obedient, and to live as a monk." By stable, Benedict means, "settled in a place," settled not just in the monastic life, but in this monastic house, with these monks and this abbot, for life. A monk could expect to leave the monastery in his coffin, but only then for the short procession to the graveyard, on the same plot of land where he had once worked and prayed.

Benedict writes of stability of place, but he has no need to write of stability of tradition or, using a word and concept unknown to him and his world, denomination. A monk might travel or work a distance from the monastery, both subjects covered in chapter 50 of Benedict's Rule, but there is no provision for a monk who travels out of the Roman Catholic Church and into another. Where would he, or any of his contemporaries— religious or lay—go? For the fifth- and sixth-century Benedict, the Roman Catholic Church, in its laws and its lands, *is* the known world.[1]

1. "The identification of the church with the whole of organized society is the fundamental feature which distinguishes the Middle Ages from earlier and later periods of history . . . There were always indeed some outsiders, even within the geographical area of western Christendom, but at best they were people with very limited rights, and at worst they had no right even to live. At best they were Jews. The lives and basic possessions of the Jews were protected by ecclesiastical law and the self-interest of princes; they could not be killed just because they were Jews; they could not be forcibly converted; their children could not be taken from them to be brought up as Christians; they could

Our known world, the world of twenty-first-century Americans, is shaped and defined not by stability, as Benedict defines it, but by mobility and by consumer choice. The premise of consumer choice is that, somewhere, the perfect fit between product and purchaser exists. It is the responsibility of the producer to offer it, the responsibility of the purchaser to find it. The 2001 American Religious Life Identification Survey estimates that one hundred fifty-nine million Americans practice Christianity.[2] The 2008 Pew Forum on Religion and Public Life estimates that of American churchgoers, "roughly 44% of Americans now profess a religious affiliation that is different from the one in which they were raised."[3]

Open the phone book of any medium to large city and turn to the yellow-pages section for "Churches." From Apostolic Assembly of the Faith in Christ Jesus, (not one of the denominations listed in the ARI Survey) to Victory World Outreach ("Todos los services estan traducidos en Espanol"), with the traditional Catholic and Protestant churches sandwiched in between, there is literally a menu of religious entrees, as religious producers seek to meet and match with religious consumers.

Are you a Lutheran hungry for electric guitars and a drum set? Holy Cross invites you to their Sunday morning "Praise Alive" service at eleven.

There will be no drum sets and electric guitars for the Lutherans at Mount Olive. They advertise their use of "The Lutheran Hymnal - 1941," emphasizing the liturgies to be found therein on "pages 5–15," as well as the exclusive use of "The King James Bible." If you have further questions, the Mount Olive Lutherans simply have the word "*conservative*" heading their yellow-pages entry.

Pulpit Rock tells us "We're Not Just Playing Church," while First United Methodist invites us to join them "*On an Epic Journey of Life*: Where Head and Heart Walk Hand in Hand." Fresh Wind Church says

---

practice their religion, so long as they did not attempt to spread it . . . If this was the case with the most privileged class of outsiders, the licensed enemies of God, not even the right to live could be allowed to those who fell away from the orthodox Christian faith and became outsiders by their own choice" (Southern, *Western Society and the Church in the Middle Ages*, 16–17).

2. Kosmin, Mayer, and Keysar, *American Religious Life Identification Survey 2001*, 12.

3. Pew Forum, "U. S. Religious Landscape Survey," 22.

simply, "Being Different Is Good," while the Evangelical Free Church explains that they are "Equipping the Saints through the systematic expository preaching of God's Word."

Lighthouse Temple, "A Miracle Church Preaching Jesus," advertises,

No book but the Bible,

No law but Love,

No creed but Christ

One Community Bible Church gets more specific yet in its promise of a scriptural basis, by offering "Verse-by-Verse Preaching."

Even the Roman Catholic parishes advertise to reach an audience. Fallen away? Holy Apostles invites you to "Come Home." Immaculate Conception Latin Mass Parish, while announcing their intention to celebrate the Mass only in Latin in their name, also uses the advertising space to assure "In Full Communion with the Vatican and the Diocese."

American churchgoers, like all Americans, make choices. We no longer prize stability of place in worship any more than we prize stability of place in the rest of our lives. Accordingly, there is a body of literature on leaving the church, as well as leaving one church and finding another. Little is written about choosing to stay, as sticking with an uncomfortable fit is never thought wise in a consumer culture. If the sweater is too tight or too loose, we return it for another, going back again and again, until we have the proper match of body and garment.

In the books on changing traditions (fundamentalists looking for an even more literal interpretation of Scripture, Protestants "going home" to Rome, feminists heading to the womyn-centric sacred grove, conservatives fleeing inclusive rites, Catholics embracing the independent seeker church), the consumerist tone prevails. The words are those of the marketplace, and, more specifically, the dressing room. Shoe shoppers speak of the "right fit," a "comfortable feel," a "good match." That's not a bad analogy: durable shoes for the pilgrimage of faith, but it falters when we rush to the purchase and ignore the prior—and more important—question of discernment. What leads one to this choosing? Who—and what—is it that bids us stay or leave? How do we learn to listen, and to obey?

Saint Paul wrote to the Galatians, in the midst of their bitter dispute over what it means to be a Christian,

> My brothers, you were called, as you know, to liberty; but be care-
> ful, or this liberty will provide an opening for self-indulgence.
> (Gal 5:13a)

Self-indulgence can be manifest in either decision, to stay or to leave, as
can true liberty.

The question of discernment is an ancient one for the Christian
church. After the apostle Paul makes his second visit to the Christian
communities in northern Galatia, he hears of a fight that threatens to destroy their young church. Paul learns that "some agitators" (1:7) there are
claiming that his authority does not come from Christ. They argue this, in
part, because Paul does not teach the necessity of circumcision for Gentile
converts (6:12). The tenor of the argument is familiar to twenty-first-
century Christians. There are those who stand against Paul as the guard-
ians and guarantors of an ancient and holy tradition. They are Jews. Jesus
was a Jew, born into a Jewish home and observing the Jewish law. For
them, to be a Christian is to be a Jew who confesses Jesus of Nazareth as
the Messiah, the Promised One of Israel. Paul's desire to allow Gentile converts to Christianity to bypass Jewish customs such as circumcision is as
shocking for his brethren as is a current preacher in some denominations
calling for the ordination of women. And, at least one of the arguments
against such radical change is as ancient as the Galatian controversy: Jesus
was a man, all of his followers were men. How could a woman represent
Christ? Substitute the word "Jew" for the word "woman" and you begin to
understand the heat and hurt of this early battle.

Familiar too, is Paul's dismay at the split. He warns the Galatian
Christians,

> If you go snapping at each other and tearing each other to pieces,
> you had better watch or you will destroy the whole community.
> (5:15)

It is not that Paul is neutral in the dispute. He has a position, asking the
dissenting Galatians, "Are you people mad? Has someone put a spell on
you, in spite of the plain explanation you have had of the crucifixion of
Jesus Christ?" (3:1). This is not the language of the mediator, but of the
advocate.

Paul argues for freedom from Mosaic ritual law, explaining that one
cannot be a "cafeteria" Jewish-Christian; to keep one law requires the

keeping of them all. As John Chrysostom writes of the Galatian controversy in his "Homily on Galatians 5:3,"

> The provisions of the law imply one another . . . Attached to circumcision are sacrifice and the observance of days. The sacrifice again entails the observance of a day and place, the place entailing many types of purification. The purification sets up a further string of varied observances. For it is not legitimate for the impure to sacrifice, to intrude upon the holy shrines or to do any such things. Therefore this commandment of the law drags along many others.[4]

Paul calls circumcision "the yoke of slavery," and writes, "if you allow yourselves to be circumcised, Christ will be of no benefit to you at all" (5:2–3).

Paul's letter to the Galatians reads like the script of an ecclesiastical schism, a "how-to" for the various factions, and, indeed, it is clear from Chrysostom's sermon that Paul's view triumphed. And yet, for all Paul's fierce advocacy, he acknowledges that he is not finally the guide. Paul is certainly sure of himself and of his place in the church. He introduces himself in the letter as

> an apostle who does not owe his authority to men or his appointment to any human being but who has been appointed by Jesus Christ and by God the Father who raised Jesus from the dead. (1:2)

Paul receives his authority from God; so, too, the community must seek its authority to act in this conflict from God. Paul urges them to look to the Holy Spirit.

It is not the Spirit of God, but self-indulgence which fuels the consumer culture. No one buys a coat thinking, "It's a little big through the shoulders, but I'm going to buy it, because it will fit my neighbor just fine. We'll share." Fit is individual, tailored to the person, to the self. If individual fit is the basis on which one decides to leave or stay in a church, one wonders what kept the Galatians together. His letter is written in response to the fact that his teaching was not a perfect fit for all of them.

Paul calls the Galatians, and us, to seek discernment in the Holy Spirit. He writes that the Spirit brings, ". . . love, joy, peace, patience, kindness, goodness, faithfulness, gentleness and self-control" (Gal 5:22b–23a).

4. Edwards, ed., *Galatians, Ephesians, Philippians,* 74.

Agreement is nowhere to be found on the list; it would seem the perfect fit is not a feature of church life.

There is no perfect fit. That does not mean that Christians in the twenty-first century are not led in and out of communions. We are a mobile people, likely to use the word "stable" only to describe a person of sound mind, not a person who has never left the acre on which he was born. The question, rather, is one not of consumer choice, but of discernment. Should I stay or should I go? How do I know?

Paul writes that the person who seeks the Holy Spirit will find the Spirit's gifts. What role, then, do love, joy, peace, patience, kindness, goodness, faithfulness, gentleness and self-control have when one asks if this communion, perhaps the one into which I was born and raised, is still the communion to which Christ is calling me? That is what we hope to discover.

1

Choice

MELISSA MUSICK NUSSBAUM

The Lord says, is what you want
The terrible free? And I say
To the Lord, Lord speak
—Mia Nussbaum, "The Chapter of the Rending in Sunder"

The Galatian church should have split in two. There were those in the church who believed that circumcision, the ancient sign of Jewish male identity, was the legitimate sign of Christian male identity as well. There were those, like the apostle Paul, who believed no Gentile convert needed to undergo circumcision in order to join the Christian church. Imagine a world with neither reliable anesthesia nor antibiotics, and the dimensions of the crisis are clear. This is no public acknowledgement of a creed or a going down into the waters of baptism; this is surgery.

The Galatians to whom Paul writes were not Jewish converts to Christianity. They were pagan converts and Paul's own disciples. Other Christian missionaries had come after Paul, preaching the necessity of male circumcision. These "Judaizers," as Paul called them, argued that the way to Christ ran through the Jerusalem temple, with all its laws and practices. Paul argues that, for Gentile converts, the Jerusalem temple, with all its laws and practices, led not to Christ, but to slavery.

The Galatians have a choice: become Jews first, and then followers of Christ, like the original apostles and brothers in Jerusalem, or follow what Paul calls "the gospel I preach to the Gentiles" (Gal 2:2b). Paul's gospel begins not with the flesh, as suggested by the physical mark of circumcision born by Jews, but with the Spirit. He asks the Galatians, "After beginning with the Spirit, are you now ending with the flesh?" (Gal 3:3b).

Paul is making his argument against those he says "who are disturbing you and [who] wish to pervert the gospel of Christ" (Gal 1:7b). He rails, "O stupid Galatians!" (Gal 3:1a) and pleads ill health (Gal 4:12a–15). He defends his position as God's position.

> Now I want you to know, brothers, that the gospel preached by me is not of human origin. For I did not receive it from a human being, nor was I taught it, but it came through a revelation of Jesus Christ. (Gal 1:1–12)

He works mightily to win, or win again, these believers to his side.

Paul knows they have a choice, to follow him or the Judaizers. He acknowledges this in the letter when he writes,

> I had been entrusted with the gospel to the uncircumcised, just as Peter to the circumcised, for the one who worked in Peter for an apostolate to the circumcised worked also in me for the Gentiles . . . (Gal 7b–8a)

There are devout Christians who are both circumcised and not, and Paul clearly wants to keep the Galatian converts he has won both Christian *and* uncircumcised.

Paul knows the Galatians have a choice, but he does not want to suggest that the choices are of equal value. Why can't pagan converts submit to Jewish law as long as they believe in the crucified and risen Christ? Paul answers by way of another question:

> Now that you have come to know God, or rather to be known by God, how can you turn back again to the weak and destitute elemental powers? Do you want to be slaves to them all over again? (Gal 4:9)

He is comparing the slavery of idolatry to the slavery of the Jewish law and offers only two positions: Christ and freedom or the Law and slavery.

How are the Galatians to make a choice? How are they to act in true liberty, as "freeborn sons"? With either choice, there will be a rendering, a tearing apart from beloved leaders and from beloved brothers and sisters.

Despite Jesus' prayer in the Gospel of John that "They may be one, as we are one, I in them and you in me" (John 17:21a), these painful splits and leave-takings, accompanied by the recriminations Paul heaps upon rival evangelists, have been part of the church since the first century.

The question is not, Will Christians leave one denomination, or tradition, for another? The question is, How does a Christian distinguish between the pew fatigue—insipid hymnody, uninspired preaching, parish snits—that makes every church-goer want to run screaming from the assembly, and the true leading of the Holy Spirit, a leading that may bring one to go, or stay? How should the choice—to leave or to remain—be made?

Theologian R. R. Reno has defended both sides of the divide. In his book, *In the Ruins of the Church,* he makes the argument for staying in the Anglican Communion.[1] Three years later, he chronicles his reception into the Catholic Church in an article, "Out of the Ruins," published in the theological journal *First Things.* Reno sees his original decision "to fight for orthodoxy in mainline Protestantism" as a stand for truth and against a culture he describes as "one of leave-taking [that] champions the seeker as the hero of the spiritual life."[2] He contrasts the mythical seeker with Benedict's Rule and its vow of stability. Reno writes,

> The sinful soul will twist and turn to elude God's grasp, and for monks, this is manifest in the all-too-human tendency to wander from place to place in an effort to find a congenial community and a sympathetic abbot.[3]

The layman's question, Reno argues, is very like the monk's:

> What are we to do in this jungle of denominationalism? Are we sinful men and women equipped to embark on a project of deciding which churches are best? When church becomes a choice, will we not guide ourselves to our own self-destruction?[4]

And yet, church *does* become a choice for Reno, when he leaves the Anglican Communion and is received into the Roman Catholic Church. But "choice," even as he freely makes one, is the concept Reno rejects:

1. Reno, *In the Ruins of the Church.*
2. Reno, "Out of the Ruins," 12.
3. Ibid., 13.
4. Ibid., 12.

> I put myself up for reception into the Catholic Church as one
> might put oneself up for adoption. A man can no more guide his
> spiritual life by his own ideas than a child can raise himself on the
> strength of his native potential.[5]

Reno uses the language of adoption, and the language of powerlessness.
Infants, and more rarely, children, are adopted. Adults are almost never
adopted, and yet Reno is an adult, chronologically and in Christ. An infant
may not be able to raise himself "on the strength of his native potential,"
but an adult can, and does. Reno is no infant, no child. He is a mature
believer, one of Paul's "freeborn sons" who has made a choice in liberty.

Why is "choice" such a scary word? The very freedom God offers to
Adam in the Garden of Eden attracts and repels us.

> You are free to eat from any of the trees of the garden except the
> tree of knowledge of good and bad. From that tree you shall not
> eat; the moment you eat from it you are surely doomed to die.
> (Gen 2:16a–17)

"You are free." Free to choose. Those are haunting words, containing, as
they do, the choices we make for life or for death.

In *Mere Christianity*, C. S. Lewis addresses the terror and delight of
human freedom:

> God created things which had free will. That means creatures
> which can go either wrong or right. Some people think they can
> imagine a creature which is free but had no possibility of going
> wrong; I cannot.
>
> If a thing is free to be good it is also free to be bad. And free
> will is what made evil possible. Why, then, did God give them
> free will? Because free will, though it makes evil possible, is also
> the only thing that makes possible any love or goodness or joy
> worth having. A world of automata—of creatures that worked like
> machines—would hardly be worth creating. The happiness which
> God designs for His higher creatures is the happiness of being
> freely, voluntarily united to Him and to each other in an ecstasy
> of love and delight compared to which the most rapturous love
> between a man and a woman on this earth is mere milk and water.
> And for that they must be free.[6]

---

5. Ibid., 16.
6. Lewis, *Mere Christianity*, 52.

Part of the problem may be linguistic. Even for Christians who accept the teaching of God's gift of free will and the choice such a gift implies, common usage affects our understanding. Certain nouns are wedded to certain modifiers. "Choice" in the twenty-first century is either "pro" or "consumer," both troublesome notions for orthodox Christians. Those modifiers cover the full range from life issues to justice issues.

"Pro-choice" means the license, for example, to choose to accept or reject the humanity of an unborn child or a comatose adult based on the needs, not of the unborn child or the comatose adult, but of the caretaker whose life will be burdened by their care.

"Consumer choice" means the license to arrange one's life according to material preference or desire. If prison labor in China means cheap silks and child labor in Indonesia means cheap running shoes, well, *I look good in silk and I'll look even better if I work out with these running shoes.*

"Pro-choice" and "consumer choice" are rooted not in God's will as received by the universal church, but in individual needs, wants, conveniences and desires. This is not to say that the Christian church heeds perfectly—or consistently, or even well—the will of God. It is to say the church knows—and is called again and again to—a standard for choice that is prior, and often counter to, the wants of any one person. The church understands choice as something that, even when exercised by the individual, affects the whole Body.

So choice itself, understood as the "liberty" to which Paul calls the Galatians, is a gift. It is the gift God offers us from the very beginning of human history.

How do we, then, in word and practice, divorce "choice" from its most common and unwelcome modifiers? How do we understand and live "choice" as holy liberty, as "freeborn sons of God"? And, perhaps most importantly, how do we exercise choice as members of the Body of Christ?

Paul writes to the Galatians that their freedom is freedom for service through love. He is not saying there aren't other forms of freedom. In fact, Paul names what he might characterize as the freedoms of the flesh:

> Immorality, impurity, licentiousness, idolatry, sorcery, hatreds, rivalry, jealousy, outbursts of fury, acts of selfishness, dissensions, factions, occasions of envy, drinking bouts, orgies, and the like. (Gal 5:19b–21a)

The list is long, and Paul's use of the phrase "and the like" suggests it could be much longer.

The freedom Christ offers is of a particular and peculiar sort. The freedom Christ offers is the liberty of the father walking the road, searching for a sign of his renegade son. It is the liberty of a father who refuses, no matter the provocation, to set his face against the son who has surely turned against him.

It is the liberty of the nailed and dying Christ: The liberty to pardon and welcome the thief, the liberty to call down mercy on the bloody hands of his killers, the liberty to care for his grieving mother, the liberty to provide for his followers, the liberty to cry out to God in a world God seems to have abandoned.

It is the liberty of service, and Paul tells us that the servant, like every living thing, will bear fruit and will be known by its fruits. The fruits of the free service in Christ, Paul says, are these:

> Love, joy, peace, patience, kindness, generosity, faithfulness, gentleness, self-control.

"Against such," he adds, "there is no law" (Gal 5:22b–23).

To better understand what Paul is saying, let's return to the father walking the road, looking for his son. In Luke's Gospel, where Jesus tells this parable, we meet a man who has done all that the law requires. He has fathered his two sons and provided for them in his household. He has accumulated an inheritance which will be theirs upon his death. The law does not require him to distribute the inheritance while he lives, and yet, when asked to do so by his greedy younger son, the father hands over half the property to him.

The younger son "set off to a distant country where he squandered his inheritance on a life of dissipation" (Luke 15:13b). The father is not expected by law to rescue his son. The son knows this, for, when he finds himself hungry and in need he realizes

> How many of my father's hired workers have more than enough food to eat, but here I am dying from hunger. I shall get up and go to my father and I shall say to him, "Father, I have sinned against heaven and against you. I no longer deserve to be called your son; treat me as you would treat one of your hired workers." (Luke 15:17b–19)

There is no expectation that he will be welcomed home as a son. He has forfeited such treatment by his shabby behavior. But the father is not acting out of the law, that sturdy wall protecting the weak from the strong and the lowly from the powerful. He has climbed over the wall, leaping every barrier that keeps him from his son. He has breached the wall out of love for his lost boy. He watches in peace and in patience. He searches in faithfulness. He awaits his son in kindness and gentleness.

God gives the law out of concern for the little ones who are everywhere swallowed up and trampled down by the mighty. God gives the law; the law does not give God. It is his servant and not his master.

The father acts in love, which is the very nature of God, and so above the law. "Against such, there is no law."

Parents know this. The legal standards for maintaining custody of one's children are spare. One must not starve or beat or abandon them. That is the law, and it is a good one. But the good father, the good mother, the parent Jesus describes in Luke 15 goes beyond the law, far beyond the merely required, and all out of a love which sees the other's need before one's own.

In the freedom of service, one is free to choose how that service will be lived. Knowing what he is asking of this young Christian community— to make a choice between teachers and friends—Paul gives them a rule, or canon, against which such choices may be measured and made. The rule can be found in his list of the fruits of the Spirit.

Is one leaving a church in which one's faction has fallen from favor? In which one's rivals are ascendant? If I stay, will I suffer a loss of power or prestige? If I stay, will I bully the dissenters whose faction lost?

The believer is free to leave, or to stay, but is he, is she, acting in the freedom of Christ? Can one leave a church in patience, led by love, and moving deeper into joy? Can one remain in a church in patience, led by love, and moving deeper into joy?

Jesus' story is instructive here. The younger son leaves the father, believing himself to have won the contest of wills. He has his inheritance and he didn't even have to wait for the old man to die. When, poor and homeless, he returns, he expects the father to treat him as badly as he was treated. One more score will be tallied and evened up.

When the father moves beyond the law into love, calling for feasting and celebration to welcome the returned rebel, the younger son is not the only one to be surprised.

> Now the older son had been out in the field and, on his way back, as he neared the house, he heard the sound of music and dancing. He called one of the servants and asked what it might mean. The servant said to him, "Your brother has returned and your father has slaughtered the fattened calf because he has him back safe and sound." He became angry and, and when he refused to enter the house, his father came out and pleaded with him. He said to his father in reply, "Look, all these years I served you and not once did I disobey your orders; yet you never gave me even a young goat to feast on with my friends. But when your son returns who swallowed up your property with prostitutes, for him you slaughter the fattened calf." (Luke 15:25–30)

The older son remembers his every obedience to the law. He remembers his brother's every transgression against the law, but he has forgotten love. And freedom that is not rooted and held fast by the fruits of the Spirit leads to freedoms that will bind and hobble us, until, like the older son, we become angry, and refuse to enter our father's house.

To Dance with God:
Family Ritual and Community Celebration
GERTRUDE MUELLER NELSON

[We] are a people, pregnant. Pregnant and waiting. We long for the God/
Man to be born and the waiting is hard. Our whole life is spent, one way
or another, in waiting. Information puts us on hold and fills our waiting
ear with thin, irritating music. Our order hasn't come in yet. The eleva-
tor must be stuck. Our spouse is late. Will the snow never melt, the rain
never stop, the paint ever dry? Will anyone ever understand? Will I ever
change? Life is a series of hopes, and waitings, and half-fulfillments . . .

Waiting, because it will always be with us, can be made a work of art,
[when we are invited] to underscore and understand with a new patience
the very feminine state of being, waiting. Our masculine world wants
to blast away waiting from our lives. Instant gratification has become
our constitutional right and delay an aberration. We equate waiting
with wasting . . . But waiting is unpractical time, good for nothing but
mysteriously necessary to all that is becoming. As in a pregnancy,
nothing of value comes into being without a period of quiet incubation:
not a healthy baby, not a loving relationship, not a reconciliation, a new
understanding, a work of art, never a transformation. Rather, a shortened
period of incubation brings forth what is not strong or whole or even
alive. Brewing, baking, simmering, fermenting, ripening, germinating,
gestating are the feminine processes of becoming and they are the
symbolic states of being which belong in a life of value, necessary to
transformation.[1]

1. Nelson, *To Dance with God*, 61–62.

17

2

Self-control

Melissa Musick Nussbaum

Like the bee, we distill poison from honey for our self-defense—what happens to the bee if it uses its sting is well known.

— Dag Hammarskjold

Paul writes to the Galatians, "For freedom Christ sets us free; so stand firm and do not submit again to the yoke of slavery" (Gal 5:1). Self-control is not freedom's enemy, but its fruit. For self-control is not the yoke another places upon us, but the yoke we place upon our own passions. The slave is constrained by another; the free person constrains herself.

I have raised five children and I am watching two of my children raise four more. They see what I saw: children are subject to their needs and appetites. A missed nap, a late supper, candy denied, a virus, any of these are sufficient to bring a child to screaming and kicking, to sobbing and collapse. I remember an afternoon many years ago, when I had three children under the age of five. I sent the older two, equipped with a plastic measuring cup, on a carefully planned errand to a neighbor's house two doors away. They were to get the cocoa I needed to make a chocolate cake. I had called my neighbor and arranged for the visit, telling her I would be waiting at the house when they returned. I walked the children to the neighbor's house, pushing their infant sister in her stroller. I gauged that I had just enough time to continue on a brisk walk around the block with the baby. I figured we would all meet back on our front porch at the same time. I miscalculated.

By the time I turned the corner to our house I could hear my little girl screaming. I broke into a run, the baby bouncing in the nylon seat.

I reached the porch and was able to hear from my son, the oldest of the three, what had happened. They had gone into the Talley's house, where Mrs. Talley had given them, not a cup of cocoa, but an entire tin. Then they walked the few yards home, and onto the porch, where they rang the bell. When I did not open the door, Abram told his sister, "Mama's not here."

Elisabeth began to cry, her tears escalating into sobs and then screams, as the seconds ticked by and I did not appear. Somehow, in her frenzy, she shook the lid off the cocoa tin and the chocolate powder began to fly. By the time I reached her, Elisabeth, her brother and the porch were covered in a fine, brown dust. Tears and mucus streaked wet trails through the grime on her face. Cocoa clung to the front window and settled into the screen covering the front door.

Elisabeth had not meant to spill the cocoa. She was proud to be entrusted with an errand and prouder still to have been given the cocoa tin to hold. None of her actions were conscious or willful. She was reacting to the dreadful sentence, "Mama's not here," led by terror and ruled by panic. She believed she had been abandoned, and she acted out of that belief.

There is an urgency in Paul's letter to the Galatians that, without self-control, might tip over into panic. Paul does not, as is his custom, give thanks for the brothers and sisters in the local church. He begins not with thanksgiving, but with rebuke, "amazed" at their behavior, a behavior he describes as "quickly forsaking the one who called you by the grace of Christ" (Gal 1:6a). He believes the Galatians have abandoned him, and more importantly, his teaching. In abandoning his teaching, Paul believes, they have abandoned Christ.

As for those, he writes, "who are disturbing you," they "wish to pervert the gospel of Christ." It is strong language, and it will grow stronger, as Paul pronounces an anathema, or curse, upon anyone—even "an angel from heaven"—who "should preach a gospel other than the one we preached to you" (Gal 1:6b–9).

Paul believes the very faith itself is at stake in Galatia. This is not a matter on which the faithful can disagree. Paul disagrees not just with sisters and brothers in Galatia, but with Peter—an apostle called by Jesus and singled out by Jesus as the rock upon whom the church will be built—on the question of circumcision. Paul uses his rebuke of Peter as an example of his constancy and courage before false teaching.

> And when Kephas (Peter) came to Antioch, I opposed him to his face because he was clearly wrong. For, until some people came from James, he used to eat with Gentiles; but when they came, he began to draw back and separated himself, because he was afraid of the circumcised. And the rest of the Jews also acted hypocritically along with him, with the result that even Barnabas was carried away by their hypocrisy. But when I saw that they were not on the right road in line with the truth of the gospel, I said to Kephas in front of all, "If you, though a Jew, are living like a Gentile and not like a Jew, how can you compel the Gentiles to live like Jews?" (Gal 2:11–14)

We are so accustomed to Paul as the apostle of the epistle that we lose sight of him as a full person, acting in the contradictions of all humankind. We have to remember that he is no stranger to violence, that Paul watched as Stephen was stoned to death. This cannot have been a quick and merciful end. Paul stood there, protecting the cloaks of the stone-throwers as he did nothing to protect Stephen from murder. The writer of Acts puts it simply, "Now Saul (Paul) was consenting to his (Stephen's) execution."

Later that same day, the writer of Acts tells us,

> There broke out a severe persecution of the church in Jerusalem and all were scattered throughout the countryside of Judea and Samaria, except the apostles. Devout men buried Stephen and made a loud lament over him. Saul, meanwhile, was trying to destroy the church; entering house after house and dragging out men and women, he handed them over for imprisonment. (Acts 8:1b–3)

The image of Paul on this rampage, breaking into houses and hauling people from their hiding places, knowing all the while what violent ends awaited them, is an uncomfortable, and perhaps unfamiliar, one for us. Most of us know about Paul as the complicit bystander, but how many remember Paul as the active persecutor? Paul reminds the Galatians of his violent history, "For you heard of my former way of life in Judaism, how I persecuted the church of God beyond measure and tried to destroy it" (Gal 1:13).

Paul is capable of rage when he believes—as he did when Stephen was martyred and as he does in the Galatian controversy—that the very truth of God is being perverted. And perhaps there is no stronger testimony to Paul's "grace of apostleship" or of his "belong(ing) to Christ Jesus," than the way in which he handles the Galatian crisis. He writes a letter. He writes a letter to the leaders of the community in conflict, and not to some other group in another city, where he could perhaps be sure of sympathy and support. He writes directly to those involved. It is an angry, and anguished, letter, to be sure. But it is as far from his Jerusalem street-fighting days as a ballpoint pen is from a rifle.

Paul truly acts a free man here, placing the yoke himself on his passions, and practicing self-control.

Self-control is not one of the sexy fruits of the Spirit. Check bulletins and sermons and retreat talks; there will be lots of talk about love, and little about self-control. Love heads Paul's list of the fruits of the Spirit; self-control is the last one he names. Yet, love without self-control soon ceases to be love at all. Consider Paul, whose love for God leads him on that terrible day in Jerusalem to acts of violence.

The writer of Second Peter speaks of self-control, among other spiritual fruits, as a kind of supplement or leaven, a vital ingredient without which other merits are lacking. The word self-control is from the Greek *enkrateia*, which means, in part, possessing power and having strength. Baking powder is tasteless and used in small amounts compared to other ingredients, but it is powerful, in that it causes a cake to rise, to be light, to have the texture we associate with cake.

> For this very reason, make every effort to supplement your faith with virtue, virtue with knowledge, knowledge with self-control, self-control with endurance, endurance with devotion, devotion with mutual affection, mutual affection with love. If these are yours and increase in abundance, they will keep you from being idle or unfruitful in the knowledge of our Lord Jesus Christ. (2 Pet 1:5–8)

And, just as a lack of leaven will leave a cake tasting flat, a lack of self-control renders the other gifts unfruitful, unproductive, and barren.

A congregation in my city split in 2007. The split was physical, as well as theological: One faction continues to worship in the parish church while the other has moved into a space donated by, and shared with, another denomination. People whose forbearers are buried on the parish grounds no longer feel welcome to visit the graves. Parents who married in the church know their own children will not be welcome to marry there. Long friendships, even family ties, have been strained, and sundered, in the congregational split. Neighbors no longer speak to one another. Lawsuits have been filed on both sides.

Nearly a year after the split, the pastor of the faction still occupying the parish church preached a sermon—posted the next day on the church website—"about our current circumstances in the parish." He begins by saying, "We are under attack. We are under spiritual and temporal attack by the devil himself, assisted by his evil and corrupt colleagues." He identifies one of the "evil and corrupt colleagues" as the local bishop, "who is himself fully in league with forces dedicated to a secular and sexual revision of the Christ's gospel."[1]

The pastor uses the words "attack" or "attacks" nine times in his sermon. He modifies the word "attack" with the adjective "devilish" twice, once referring to the former organist. "Evil is real—and we are in its sights—and its minions are legion and on the attack," he says, and continues, describing these attacks as something of which "only devil inspired evil people" would be capable.[2]

He uses as his text the account of the healing of the Gerasene demoniac from the eighth chapter of Luke's gospel. He paraphrases the pericope and says, "Then the demons came out of the man and entered the pigs, and the herds rushed down the steep bank and into the lake and were drowned."[3]

In Luke's account it is Jesus who allows the demons to leave the man's body and enter the herd of swine, the unclean entering the unclean. It is Jesus who has the authority to command the demons. A clear distinction is made between the man and the demons in him, just as a clear distinction is made between the man's helplessness and Jesus' authority. The man is left not only unharmed after the demons depart, but healed, and "in his right mind," as the gospel puts it.

But this pastor realigns the characters in Luke's story. He identifies the demons with the men and women in the faction still loyal to the local

---

1. Armstrong, "Under Attack!!!"

2. Ibid.

3. Ibid.

bishop, and states the necessity for sending the demons "away from us over the cliff and into the sea." The members of the other faction are not helpless hosts for evil, but, as he says, "devil inspired evil people," and "evil and corrupt colleagues" of the devil. A colleague, it is important to remember, is a fellow worker, one willing to work and committed to the task.

He identifies himself and his followers with Christ, in whose hands is the authority to call and cast out the demons, without, in Luke's account, ever harming the man in whose body the demons found refuge. The pastor says, "Yes, we need to name, as Jesus did, the evil among us and we need to send it over the cliff." Near the end of the sermon he sounds this note again, inviting the assembly to a parish meeting. He tells them, "And so we have named the enemy . . . and (at) our meeting this morning (we) will lay out our plan to run them over the cliff."[4]

If the distinction between the demons and the host in Luke's gospel is lost, then the ones to be driven "down the steep bank into the lake and . . . drowned" are not spirits, but people, men and women. They will not be unharmed, as in the gospel, but drowned.

Like Paul with the Galatians, this pastor believes the truth of the gospel is at stake. Like Paul, he is passionate in defense of his teaching. But is he, like Paul, placing the yoke of self-control upon his passions? Notice that Paul, early in this letter, acknowledges his own capacity for evil. He minces no words "I persecuted the church of God and tried to destroy it" (Gal 1:13a). It is a stark confession, offered with neither excuse nor explanation. There is no doubt that Paul can, and has been, led astray, the very claim he levels against "some who are disturbing you and wish to pervert the gospel of Christ." He identifies *with* Christ, but not *as* Christ, in this, or any, situation. In contrast, the pastor in my city claims nothing but good will and faithfulness on his part or on the part of his congregation. "But always," he says,

> where one is doing God's good work, the Devil's radar goes off, and he musters his forces, even seducing good people to do his bidding. So with every success we have had over the years we have experienced certain devilish attacks of pettiness, bickering, jealousy, hurt feelings, gossip, resentment—all those tools the devil uses to undermine good.[5]

4. Ibid.
5. Ibid.

Common sense and personal experience tells us that all humans involved in conflict, whether in the right or the wrong, are capable of pettiness, bickering, jealousy, hurt feelings, gossip and resentment. Humans in healthy and peaceful church communities are prone to the same hateful impulses. Yet, speaking of bickering and "all those tools the devil uses to undermine good," the pastor states, "But we named that evil when it reared its ugly head, driving it from our midst." There, be lions; here, only lambs.

Self-control demands self-truth and self-examination. We are not angels; neither are we gods, but all, as Paul writes in the third chapter of his letter to the Romans, "have sinned and fallen short of the glory of God" (Rom 3:23b). It is a sign of Paul's self-control that he acknowledges his own faults in the letter to the community he chastises. And it is no coquettish pout, but a frank and honest statement of his own serious sin, sin from which no believer is immune. Paul accuses Peter and the Galatians of wrongdoing, but he also accuses himself.

Then, consider the method by which the pastor's message is delivered. It is difficult, if not impossible, to compare the communications of the twenty-first century with the first, but there are some comparisons we can take into account. The pastor's sermon was not addressed to his dissident brethren; it was, quite literally, preaching to the choir, those who have, by their presence, made their allegiance with him, and to him, plain. Paul writes his harsh letter to the ones he means to correct, and, thereby, save. He does not seek out a sympathetic audience, but takes his argument to those with whom he so bitterly disagrees. He is not looking for applause, but conversion.

It is understandable to desire allies in a dispute, but self-control demands that those who do not need to be brought into the fray be left alone. By posting the sermon on the website—without any word from the other faction—the pastor widens the net of strife. Jesus addresses church conflict in Matthew:

> If your brother sins against you, go and tell him his fault between you and him alone. If he listens to you, you have won over your brother. If he does not listen, take one or two others along with you, so that every fact may be established on the testimony of two or three witnesses. If he refuses to listen to them, tell the church. If he refuses to listen even to the church, then treat him as you would a Gentile or a tax collector. (Matt 18:15–17)

We can wonder about the meaning of the last sentence, given that Matthew was a tax collector chosen as a disciple, and that within fifty years after Jesus' death and resurrection the church is welcoming Gentiles. But what is plain is the sense that details of disputes should be confined to those church members whose involvement is necessary for a fair hearing and just resolution.

If self-control demands self-truth and self-knowledge, then it must begin with self-examination. And self-examination, for the Christian, begins with the realization that there is a God, and I am not He. Only God is without sin or stain. Only God is without change or contradiction. That leaves me knowing that I do sin, that I am stained, and that no act of mine is completely innocent or free of self-interest. I may well see the splinter in my sister's eye and be offended by it, but I am not allowed to overlook the wooden beam in my own. Nor am I allowed to pretend that the splinter in my brother's eye is different in kind from my beam: Both wood, both unwelcome. We are both of us sinners in need of the Christ's healing.

Excerpt from Book 20, *On Patience*

CYPRIAN OF CARTHAGE

The virtue of patience extends widely and its wealth and abundance proceed from a source that has indeed a single name, but with its full-flowing streams it is diffused through many glorious courses, and nothing in our actions can avail towards the full realization of merit which does not take the power for its accomplishment from that source. It is patience that both commends us to God and saves us for God. It is that same patience which tempers anger, bridles the tongue, governs the mind, guards peace, rules discipline, breaks the onslaught of lust, suppresses the violence of pride, extinguishes the fire of dissension, restrains the power of the wealthy, renews the endurance of the poor in bearing their lot, guards the blessed integrity of virgins, the difficult chastity of widows, and the indivisible love of husbands and wives. It makes men humble in prosperity, brave in adversity, meek in the face of injuries and insults. It teaches us to pardon our offenders quickly; if you yourself should offend, it teaches you to ask pardon often and with perseverance. It vanquishes temptations, sustains persecutions, endures sufferings and martyrdoms to the end. It is this patience which strongly fortifies the foundations of our faith. It is this patience which sublimely promotes the growth of hope. It directs our action, so that we can keep to the way of Christ while we make progress because of His forbearance.[1]

---

1. In *Ante-Nicene Fathers.*

3

Faithfulness

JANA MARGUERITE BENNETT

All things living He doth feed; His full hand supplies their need:
For His mercies shall endure, Ever faithful, ever sure.

– John Milton

The way we Christians often use the word "faith" makes it seem like a commodity. Faith is an item you either possess or you don't. The question, "Do you have faith in Jesus?" is asked as a way to find out whether you have this particular, essential item or not, similar to the way you might call a neighbor and ask whether he or she has sugar that you can borrow.

This idea of faith is often tied to propositions, such as whether one believes that Jesus died for humanity's sins or whether God created heaven and earth. If you agree with the propositions, then you can safely answer yes, I do have faith. Assent to propositions becomes a true/false test for making determinations about faith. All these propositions taken together are sometimes referred to as "the Christian faith." In our minds, faith is often an intellectual assent and a private internal motion that we personally have toward Christianity.

We do use the word "faith" in other ways that suggest much more complexity than simple intellectual assent. There is faith in terms of fidelity, for instance, as in whether a spouse is faithful or unfaithful to marriage vows. We use the word to speak of some kind of belief and stake in an unknown, but good outcome in a distant future ("I have faith that this situation will turn out all right"). In both of these contexts, faith is not an object, but a way of living. Being a faithful spouse entails certain actions toward one's husband or wife, and not simply an intellectual assent to the marriage. Having a belief in some good outcome entails, in part, that one live as though that good outcome were possible. As one common sermon reference to faith puts it: "If you pray for rain, why don't you bring an umbrella?"

The Scriptures, too, demonstrate more complexity in the use of "faith." Much of the time, the use of the word "faithful" is in conjunction with God's faithfulness and not humanity's. In the letter to the Romans, Paul writes about how human faith in God has nothing to do with God's faithfulness toward *us*. If no one has faith, God would still be faithful (Rom 3:3). Psalm 136 recites all of the ways in which God has acted with favor toward the Israelites, and after each brief statement, there is the refrain: "God's steadfast love endures forever." By the end of this long psalm, the very repetition of the refrain reminds us of God's faithfulness, his steadfastness, and his enduring love for us.

God's demonstrated faithfulness to us implies a resounding call for us to return that faithfulness to God. The prophets of the Old Testament are full of these reminders—especially in the context of the Israelites' unfaithfulness to God, worship of other gods, and sheer laziness. The prophet Jeremiah says, "The Lord said to me, 'Have you seen what the faithless Israel has done? She has gone up on every high hill and under every spreading tree and committed adultery there'" (Jer 3:6). Later the prophet proclaims, "I will give them a heart to know me, that I am the Lord. They shall be my people and I shall be their God, for they shall return to me with all their heart" (Jer 24:7). Isaiah, too, says, "Return to me, for I have redeemed you" (Isa 44:22).

Perhaps it is in the memory of Israel's unfaithfulness that Jesus offers parables about remaining steadfast even when the reason for faith is not readily apparent. In a parable from Luke's Gospel, the parable about the steward, Jesus cautions that those who manage the master's household while he is away ought to care for it as though the master himself were taking care of the household. Such a steward is contrasted with the one who says, "The master is a long time in coming" and then beats the servants and takes liberties with the food and drink of the house. Jesus says that the first steward, the faithful one, will inherit all, while the second steward will receive just punishment (Luke 12:42–48). These parables imply that faithfulness to God requires living and working for God steadfastly in the way that God requires.

Thus, deeper considerations of faith and faithfulness suggest that this fruit of the Spirit is not just an intellectual assent to belief. Faithfulness requires faithful living—a demonstration of faith. One of the points we as authors consider throughout this book is the way in which the fruits are gifts given to us by God and which must be lived and manifested in Christian community. The connection between these two is especially apparent for the gift of faithfulness, as we shall see.

The thirteenth-century theologian Thomas Aquinas writes in his treatise on the Fruits of the Spirit: "[As] to his suffering with equanimity the evils his neighbor inflicts on him . . . to this pertains faith, if we take it as denoting fidelity. But if we take it for the faith whereby we believe in God, then man is directed thereby to that which is above him, so that he subject his intellect and, consequently, all that is his, to God" (*Summa Theologiae* IaIIae Q. 70, *art. 3 resp.*).

Thomas notes that fidelity to neighbors is one part of faithfulness—a particular kind of fidelity. He suggests that faithfulness is what we do even in the face of evil done to us. The second consideration of faith seems somewhat like the intellectual assent first considered above, but Thomas extends that to say that because there is intellectual assent, therefore our entire beings and all that we possess is directed toward God. For Thomas, faith is both action and intellectual assent. Moreover, he considers that we have faith both in relation to our neighbors as well as to God.

Faithfulness to neighbors is important, especially for upholding Christian community. We often speak of other peoples' faithfulness in relation to ourselves. We notice the people who stick by us when an unwelcome diagnosis of cancer comes our way (a time when many "friends" leave), or when there is a death or loss of a job, and we call these people faithful and "true Christians" who live out their faith. Fidelity in the face of danger and distress is a highly prized gift and virtue. We admire those friends who stick with us "through thick and thin" more than we admire the flighty ones.

The parable of the Good Samaritan is, in part, about faithfulness (though we are prone to think of this parable as being about love of all our neighbors, and not faithfulness). In the traditional way the story goes, you would expect that the priest or the Levite would stop and help their fellow compatriot, but they pass along on the other side of the road, too busy with their own affairs. The Samaritan, an outcast in terms of the Jewish community, is the one who sees the beaten man as his neighbor, despite social assumptions about who was whose true "neighbor." Love has no bounds, so the telling goes.

But the parable tells also about the kind of love that we are commanded to practice, and it involves faithfulness. The Samaritan is faithful to the person he stopped to help and he is faithful to his own actions in beginning to care for the robbed man. That is, he did not stop to help, get into the middle of helping, and then change his mind. The Samaritan is faithful despite inconvenience, and despite having no assurance that his time and money would be repaid.

In this gospel narrative, fidelity is closely related to the practice of love. And fidelity, rightly practiced, is done despite inconvenience, despite lack of thanks, despite the beaten man's lack of funds. Thomas Aquinas takes this fruit of the Spirit even further: faithfulness is a fruit you have even in the face of hardship and evil.

It is therefore a very serious undertaking for a Christian who, after all, is to be about living a life of love, to leave a Christian community even for another Christian community. What are the grounds on which a Christian might faithfully leave a community? In part, because faithfulness resides in community, it is the community that can and should tell us what unfaithful behavior is. And Christian communities do tell us. For example, leaving due to a job change or family difficulty is usually seen as a faithful leaving; it is sad for all concerned, but it is not seen as unfaithful. But leaving due to differences in theology, or differences over leadership, or budget crises are more commonly seen (at least among those being left) as an unfaithful move. I think here of the member of the vestry who leaves in the middle of a budget crisis because he just doesn't want to deal with the arguments anymore; I think of the family with teenagers who leaves due to a fallout with the youth minister.

I grew up United Methodist and wondered, off and on, whether to become Episcopalian, Presbyterian, or even Catholic. I struggled with whether to leave or stay in my United Methodist Church for eight years and one of the central questions in that time was about fidelity. How *could* I consider leaving these people who had nurtured me and formed me and brought me up? I thought they would see leaving them as a betrayal and rejection and I didn't want that for these people whom I loved. I worried that it *was*, in fact, a betrayal and rejection of them. I was also very involved in the United Methodist Church—I was a member of several national boards and agencies and was a delegate to General Conference, the denomination's highest decision-making body. People had elected me to these positions out of good will and the belief that I was a true and loyal member. Leaving loomed as a faithless action.

I had also been brought up by parents and grandparents who believed that being faithful or loyal to a cause was a virtue, and it indicated the degree of trust and hope that you put in God. I remember my grandmother raising eyebrows at the groups of people that would leave her local church en masse every time a new pastor came into town because they didn't like his preaching or his high-handed (or hands-off, depending) way of running the parish council. "I don't go to church to worship the pastor; I go to church to worship the Lord!" she would say, in a fierce, determined voice. A person who left a church because the pastor didn't measure up was, on my grandmother's view, a person who didn't trust in the Lord enough and didn't have his or her priorities in the right place.

Thus, I feared that leaving the church where I grew up would be an act of unfaithfulness to the community, akin to adultery. Adultery is an act of faithlessness because it is a betrayal of the vows of fidelity that one has made to one's community. In the case of marriage, those vows are made both within the community of two that is officially joined together, but also the community gathered that witnesses the vows the couple makes. The Samaritan in Jesus' parable had not made any vows, but was faithful nonetheless.

How could I, who *had* made vows, do any less? I had made vows to the church in which I grew up: at my youth confirmation, I promised to uphold the church by my prayers, my presence, my gifts, and my service. And I did all of these, to the best of my ability. I was involved in youth group and committee work, and I read the scripture lessons in church. I was one of the "good" kids who always wanted to preach and help out. I gave what I was able to give, for someone who had a part-time, after-school job that paid minimum wage. Just like the first newlywed year of marriage often is, my youthful relationship with my Christian community was a happy one. The congregation loved me and I loved them. I learned, among them, that faithfulness was, in part, about abiding in and supporting that community.

Concern for fidelity, as faithfulness to one's neighbors, should indeed make it very difficult to discern whether to stay in or leave a Christian community. When Paul writes that one of the gifts of the Spirit is faithfulness, it is a statement against the easy way out and against faithlessness to community. The easy way for the Galatians would have been to split over the issue of circumcision and not to work at the relationships the entire congregation shared with each other.

Community is not an end in itself, however, and faithfulness to a community can become problematic. Blind fidelity to a community leads to terribly wrong situations such as blind adherence to state-sponsored churches that perpetuate state-sponsored problems and terrible splits in denominations over slavery and similar issues. In China, for example, underground Christians often mobilize for political action against the government's refusal to acknowledge non-state religions. Underground Christians have been arrested and tortured, while their Christian brothers and sisters belonging to the state-sponsored churches stand by. In the nineteenth century, several US denominations split, not over doctrine, but over the question of slavery and relationships with African-Americans; an example is the early nineteenth-century split between the Methodist Episcopal Church and the African Methodist Episcopal Church. White members adhered blindly to their communities' assumptions without thinking through either John Wesley's injunctions against slavery or Richard Allen's (the founder of the AME Church) arguments.

Faith in God, the second aspect of the fruit of faithfulness, can balance these negative aspects of faithfulness to community. Dietrich Bonhoeffer, a Lutheran pastor in Germany who was executed for his attempts to undermine Hitler's regime, wrote extensively about the demands of faith in his book *The Cost of Discipleship*. In this book, Bonhoeffer does an extended meditation on Mark 2:14—"As he was walking along, he saw Levi son of Alphaeus sitting at the tax booth, and he said to him, 'Follow me.' And he got up and followed him." Bonhoeffer is struck by the fact that Jesus' call to discipleship does not result in a profession of faith—a sort of intellectual assent. Levi does not say, "Oh, clearly you are the Son of God and I believe." No, rather, the response Levi makes is a response of obedience. Levi leaves behind everything in his life—his job, his money, his wife, his family, his synagogue, his town—everything in order to follow Jesus.

And Levi is not necessarily following Jesus on the basis of good cat-echetical methods, either. Jesus is teaching the crowds in v. 13, but Mark does not say that Levi was in the crowd, nor does it say that others in the crowd also followed Jesus. Mark gives us a stark picture: Jesus bids Levi follow him, and he does. Bonhoeffer says that the response of obedience that Levi gives is the only right and good response. "The call implies that there is only one way of believing on Jesus Christ, and that is by leaving all and going with the incarnate Son of God."[1]

Bonhoeffer continues by saying that all it takes is just one step in faith, for by taking that step one learns how to believe. If Levi had stayed behind and refused to follow Jesus, he would not have learned how to put faith in Jesus. "He who is called must go out of his situation in which he cannot believe, into the situation in which, first and foremost, faith is possible."[2] Bonhoeffer contends that having faith in God is not first about intellectual assent and emotional response—these come later. The first step in having faith is to respond to God's call by putting yourself directly on the path where you must rely on God alone.

We use peer pressure, rationalizations, and chances for advancement and public recognition as means for avoiding that singular faith in God Bonhoeffer describes. But there are all sorts of examples in history where a person has perceived that following the will of God means going against the wisdom of even the community that is led by God. Bonhoeffer is an example himself: in refusing to declare for the state-sponsored church, he was deprived of his work, his home, and eventually, his life. Oscar Romero, archbishop of El Salvador, ultimately refused to kowtow to the political machine that had essentially put him into office, instead opting for radical solidarity with the poor. Martin Luther turned away from his scholastic heritage and his monastery because he believed that God wanted him to reform the injustices of the Catholic Church; eventually he left the community altogether. La Roy Sunderland, Orange Scott, and George Storrs were among some of the earliest Methodist abolitionists working against slavery in their communities, though their work provoked intense debate and violence. Just as we deemed being faithful to community difficult, so being faithful to God is difficult because it can mean turning your back on all you have known. God can and does give commands to leave behind

---

1. Bonhoeffer, *The Cost of Discipleship*, 62.
2. Ibid.

communities, families, jobs, and friends. Deciding to leave a community or stay there should hinge on faithfulness to God.

But the decision of leaving or staying is not quite as simple as that sounds. It would be *too* simplistic to say that leaving a community is "okay" so long as one is faithful to God. The common thinking is that because God should have priority of place, we should therefore prioritize what we do according to where God leads us, regardless of other people or other commitments. The easy answer is, "God led me to do this act of leaving community, which makes the brokenness and betrayal I am leaving behind okay because I am acting in faith toward God."

There are at least two problems with this view. One problem is that not every spirit and not every nudge that we think comes from God actually comes from God. The first letter of John shows this well, for it says: "Beloved, do not believe every spirit, but test the spirits to see whether they are from God; for many false prophets have gone out into the world. By this you know the Spirit of God: every spirit that confesses that Jesus Christ has come in the flesh is from God, and every spirit that does not confess Jesus is not from God" (1 John 4:1). This writer of the New Testament, at least, knew that people could be fooled into thinking that something was good even if it was bad. We would not want to be unfaithful to a community because we had followed the command of what we thought was God, but which turned out to be some other voice.

The second problem with being too simplistic about following God over community is that God cares about fidelity to one's community, and in fact sees it as an act of faithfulness. This is because faithfulness is connected to the unity of the church as well as to love of neighbor. The Old Testament books of the prophets brim with commands to turn back to the Jewish community and be God's people once more. Jesus prays for the unity of Christians, that they may not be separated from each other. Time and time again, Paul begs the early Christians not to fight with each other but to lay aside their complaints in favor of a greater unity in Christ.

The Christians' ability to be in community in Christ is centered on love. The first letter of John says, "We know love by this, that he laid down his life for us—and we ought to lay down our lives for one another. How does God's love abide in anyone who has the world's goods and sees a brother or sister in need and yet refuses help?" (1 John 3:21–24). This letter writer sees a direct connection between the love we know in Christ's death and resurrection, and the love we strive for in Christian community. Therefore, we cannot glibly do something that might cause feelings of hurt or betrayal and assume that the other peoples' pain is somehow all right because we have a vested interest in following God.

Moreover, God has given particular sanction to the Christian community to be Christ's Body the church, and as this Body, it is representative (often imperfectly) of Christ. Paul compares the church with the body at several points. In his letter to the Romans, he writes, "For as in one body we have many members, and not all the members have the same function, so we, who are many, are one body in Christ, and individually we are members one of another. We have gifts that differ according to the grace given to us: prophecy, in proportion to faith; ministry, in ministering; the teacher, in teaching; the exhorter, in exhortation; the giver, in generosity; the leader, in diligence; the compassionate, in cheerfulness" (Rom 12:4–8).

Paul takes special care in this letter to remind people to care for each other and help each other out. He recognizes that we are not all the same, nor do we have the same function, and each of us thus brings good and diverse gifts. If one of these gifts is not present, that Christian community cannot fully be what it is. As Paul writes in another letter:

> The eye cannot say to the hand, "I have no need of you," nor again the head to the feet, "I have no need of you." . . . But God has so arranged the body, giving the greater honor to the inferior member, that there may be no dissension within the body, but the members may have the same care for one another. If one member suffers, all suffer together with it; if one member is honored, all rejoice together with it. (1 Cor 12:21, 24b–26)

"God has so arranged the body," says Paul. We are needed in our communities precisely because God has made us to have a particular place in the body. When we leave that place and that community, we leave a hole (whether we acknowledge it or not). It is no small thing for us to claim that God is not, in fact, making us members of *this* Christian community, but is in fact sending us to be members of *that* parish.

The Christian community lays a particular claim on its people that other kinds of communities do not because it is created and endowed by God. Faith in God and fidelity to community are intertwined. If we are known by our fruits, we are known by both our faith in God *and* our faithfulness to the Christian communities God has given to us.

So, how are we to reconcile the fact that God might call us out of our communities into a new life, with the fact that God *also* calls us to be faithful to a particular Christian community? How are we to know, as well, whether it is God calling us to stay or leave, or whether it is some "other spirit" that it not God?

Because of these questions, it is important to examine the intention for leaving a community to see whether the purpose is directed toward faithfulness. Above, I gave examples of people who followed God at the risk of losing significant family, national, and church communities; these people have one other point in common. Ultimately, their faithfulness to God demonstrated faithfulness *to* community as well, though it may have been difficult to see that faithfulness to the church at the time.

Bonhoeffer sought for German Christians to live truthfully rather than following a regime that led them toward a false unity and hope in an Aryan race. Luther's call for reformation was heard by the Catholic Church; the church did move toward reform with the Council of Trent. What these people hold in common is that their acts of faithlessness to their varied communities show faithfulness in wanting those same communities to be faithful to God as well. The faithfulness of these individual witnesses to God had the purpose of generating greater communal faithfulness to God, even when these people left their communions.

The fruit of faithfulness ultimately must involve the faithfulness of *both* the community *and* the individual to each other and to God. Individual Christians have the responsibility, as members of the Body, to help that Body be faithful; the Body, in turn, helps its members be faithful. So, it seems that a faith-filled person generally will not leave his or her community out of individualistic concerns. That is to say, the involvement of the community will be present somehow in that discernment. Leaving a community without telling anyone, so that you can quietly go to the church that has the more vibrant pastor or the better Sunday School program, does not demonstrate a lot of faithfulness. There are times when leaving a community is done out of a concern for individual needs, but such leaving can be done in the context of faithful living and witness. I think here of some friends of mine who are parents of an autistic child. They left the small church of which they were a part so that their son could attend the Montessori-based Sunday School program at the larger church a couple miles away because the teachers there were trained to teach kids like him. But even that decision to leave was done with the knowledge of all in the community.

The concern, from each member's point of view, must be for the Christian community as a whole, just as the concern from the Christian community's point of view must be for the member's ability to be faithful. Because of the close connection between faith in God and faithfulness to the church, being faithful likely means that one will seek out the advice and help of Christians from *both* the congregation one wants to leave and the congregation one wants to join.

It would be far more appropriate for readers to ask the community I left whether or not I was faithful to them. But here is my account of my attempt to be faithful to the community as well as to God. When I considered leaving the church in which I grew up, I talked with a lot of members from that church about whether I should leave. Doing this scared me, because I didn't want to hurt or offend people and I didn't want them to be angry at me. (Some were, some weren't.) To my great surprise, a *lot* of people that took the time to talk with me were familiar with the struggle of whether to stay or leave because they had thought about it themselves. I had been expecting that I was the only one who had really considered leaving or staying, and it was humbling, really, to discover that I wasn't the only one. But moreover, I benefited from other members' experience with the struggle to leave or stay. This, I think, is part of the point of faithfulness in community: to realize that the community is stronger than you think it is and has more to say to you than you might initially think it does.

I told these people that my reasons for leaving were largely about worship. When I went away to college and graduate school, I fell in love with Divine Liturgy, with weekly Holy Communion, because that is where I experienced God. The church in which I grew up had neither of these. It did have a ritual pattern, but one based on the camp revivals of the nineteenth century. Sermons were the last and best part of worship on Sundays at that church. Holy Communion was done monthly, but if it had to be skipped due to some other obligations, that was fine with the people. At first, I was so concerned about remaining faithful to the community that I decided I needed to "reform" my congregation and make it more liturgical—to move it away from its nineteenth-century past.

Some of the parishioners I consulted asked why I felt the need to make the church more liturgical and why I even thought that church members would be amenable to reforms in the first place. The largest example of this was my increasing devotion to Mary; I had begun to visit Marian chapels to pray, and I figured that those I had grown up with ought to also become more Marian. But Protestants I grew up with were not interested in Mary, at least not in the way I was interested in Mary. With their help, I realized that my desire to make the church into the image of what I wanted it was so much in line with contemporary consumerism. I wanted the community to be all about me and my needs. Gradually I realized that the church of my youth had its own traditions, traditions which were fruitful for people and which were not in need of reform from their own point of view. I also came to understand, with their help, that it was a form of faithlessness to want to so change the tradition as to make it unrecognizable to the people who were as much a part of the community as I was because I was no longer being faithful to the community. One pastor even gave me the names and numbers of some Catholic and Orthodox friends of hers, because she thought that I might be called to join one of those communities instead.

Ultimately, I would say that it was as much the community's choice as mine, whether to leave or to stay. My original community recognized, with great generosity, that I would be unable to be faithful in significant ways to them. They helped me, as well, to discern whether God was truly at work in this leave-taking or not.

The fruit of faithfulness is about recognizing that you have only limited control over things in this life; even "choosing" a Christian community is not really an autonomous choice in the way we usually think of choices. Though God does speak to people individually, God also works through Christian communities to move and guide people, and to confirm the words that individuals have received from God.

Faith in God has led people to do strange, almost incomprehensible things, as we saw with Romero and Bonhoeffer. Faith in community means putting your trust in people—admittedly a scary prospect in our world. But these two ways of practicing faith may be exactly what it means to "walk by faith and not by sight." Faith as intellectual assent suggests that we know certain graspable ideas; faith as a way of life is much less certain.

A Plain Account of Christian Perfection

John Wesley

Watch and pray continually against pride. If God has cast it out, see that it enter no more: It is full as dangerous as desire. And you may slide back into it unawares, especially if you think there is no danger of it. "Nay, but I ascribe all I have to God." So you may, and be proud nevertheless. For it is pride, not only to ascribe anything we have to ourselves, but to think we have what we really have not . . .

To imagine none can teach you but those who are themselves saved from sin is a very great and dangerous mistake. Give not place to it for a moment. It would lead you into a thousand other mistakes, and that irrecoverably . . .

[Always] be ready to own any fault you have been in. If you have at any time thought, spoke, or acted wrongly, be not backward to acknowledge it. Never dream that this will hurt the cause of God: no, it will further it. Be therefore open and frank, when you are taxed with anything: Do not seek either to evade or disguise it. But let it appear just as it is, and you will thereby not hinder, but adorn the Gospel.[1]

1. Wesley, "On Christian Perfection," 360.

4

Gentleness

JANA MARGUERITE BENNETT

Our brokenness is the wound through which the full power of God can penetrate our being and transfigure us in God.

– Jean Vanier

I suspect if I asked my students at this all-men's college what it means to be gentle, they might say it is a "girly" virtue. Gentleness is equated with mild-manneredness—someone always good-natured, always happy, always willing to go with the flow, someone who is a bit weaker, perhaps, because the ungentle person will be the strong, aggressive, manly type. That kind of gentleness would not seem to have much of a place in a conversation about coming and going. Indeed, viewing gentleness in this always-good-mannered light might make it seem that one could never, ever leave a community. In some of these chapters, I tend to push more toward staying with a congregation if at all possible, but I think that in this chapter, the fruit of gentleness actually requires that we take seriously that leaving is the best course of action. Gentleness is not about being blown by whatever wind happens along but is about having firm resolve in a way that does not require weakness.

Staying and going might well be taken as "winning" or "losing," depending on the reasons. Switching for the sake of a marriage might seem less like a win, while switching because of theological views definitely feels like a win. On one view, it might seem that there are winners and losers: the "winner" is the congregation who "gets" the person converting; the loser is the one who is out. This is especially the case when conversion involves people who do, in fact, have power: theologians who leave one congregation for another; pastors, ministers and priests who leave; entire congregations that leave. And in such a situation, it might seem that the side with the "numbers" is the winning side, the side with the "right" view of things. Perhaps, too, the person doing the leaving feels that there is a punitive act in all this: "I'll show them" by leaving. In this situation, it is quite easy to revert to the idea that one side wins and one side loses. The way that things often get done is through peoples' insistence that something be done "my way." In the modern world, the Nietzschean "will to power" seems to work. The one with the power is the one who wins.

Of course, Christians hear that Christ, as the exemplar, shows power does not equate with winning. One familiar way to tell the Jesus story is to tell it in terms of power: a small baby born in a backwater town manages to escape the clutches of the powerful Herodian government. Later in his life, he even shows that a humiliating death on a cross conquers death and overturns the power structures of the Roman Empire and any subsequent human creations of power. As Mary proclaims in her Magnificat: "My soul glorifies the Lord . . . [for he] pulls tyrants from their thrones and raises up the humble." This is nonsensical, paradoxical to many. Most of my students see themselves as destined for law, medicine, politics, CEOs of corporations, and the like. They see themselves as movers and shakers, and while many of them would say they are Christian, they would not say that they themselves ought to act as Christ did when he went to the cross. "There's a time and place for being the underdog," they sometimes tell me, "but if Christians really want to get things done, they need the powerful people." Lack of power, even apparent lack of power as in Christ's own humbling himself on the cross, does not seem like a viable option.

The point is not ridding the world of power but changing the view of power, and the view of what counts as powerful. Even so, it is a hard sell. In what way can gentleness even be considered a gift? And particularly when leaving a church or staying in a church can involve all sorts of plays of power, how can the gift of gentleness help a person use power rightly?

It is helpful to consider the places where gentleness is referred to in Scripture. The Greek word in Paul's letter is *praotēs*, commonly acknowledged to be difficult to describe in English equivalents. Cowardice and weakness might go along with definitions of gentleness or meekness in my students' eyes, but it really has no place in the Greek rendition. The word itself is an ancient word; it is found in Homer, for example. Aristotle's view of "gentleness" sees it as a virtue halfway between excessive anger and indifference. One who is gentle could therefore be angry at times, but compliant at others, and the rightness of his or her action depended in part on the manner, intention, and situation of the action.[1] The use of the word was not taken to mean weakness, and by all appearances, does not mean weakness when later New Testament authors use it either.

Consider some of the other passages where Paul uses the word *praotēs*. In 1 Corinthians 4, Paul encounters a scene that would be familiar today. He suggests that apostles who are following the gospel are seen as fools, reviled by the world, the "dregs of all things." Their work for Christ has caused their present situation because the suspicious world will not tolerate these "fools." By contrast, the Corinthians appear to be living the good life, believing themselves to be wise and knowledgeable about being Christian, even to the point of being quite arrogant. These Corinthians have become divided, some standing for Paul, some for Apollos, and each side believing that theirs is the correct side. In sharp response, Paul admonishes the community, saying that they cannot pass judgment on each other for they do not even know what wrongs they are committing. Then in v. 21 he writes, "But I will come to you soon, if the Lord wills, and I will find out not the talk of these arrogant people but their power. For the Kingdom of God depends not on talk but on power. What would you prefer? Am I to come to you with a stick, or with love in a spirit of gentleness?"

Paul has a contrast here with talk and power. The Corinthians may arrogantly see themselves as having power but Paul tries to mitigate that sense, suggesting that the arrogant ones are really only full of talk. True power cannot be had on the basis of arrogance, or having things, or believing that one has the "right." Paul suggests that even he himself does not know how God might view his own actions; not even he, the one who has passed along the faith to the Corinthians, can have such arrogant assurance of his correctness. The discipline Paul will mete out to the Corinthians in the last verse follows in a parallel manner—he can come to them with a stick, necessary against the arrogance that they display, or

---

1. Aristotle, *Nichomachean Ethics*, 1125b31–32.

he can come to them with gentleness, in consonance with conversion to humility.

A similar distinction between worldly power and divine power comes in Paul's second letter to the Corinthians. "I myself, Paul, appeal to you by the meekness (*praotēs*) and gentleness (*epikeias*) of Christ . . . " (2 Cor 10:1). This first verse in itself might not seem surprising except for how Paul follows with what he therefore means by being meek. "I ask that when I am present I need not show boldness by daring to oppose those who think we are acting according to human standards. Indeed, we live as human beings, but we do not wage war according to human standards" (2 Cor 10:2–3). The gentleness to which Christians are called does not have to do with a lack of power but rather of seeing power in a wholly different view. Later, Paul proclaims, "We do not dare to classify or compare ourselves with some of those who commend themselves. But when they measure themselves by one another, and compare themselves with one another, they do not show good sense. We, however, will not boast beyond limits, but will keep within the field that God has assigned to us, to reach out even as far as you" (2 Cor 10:12–13). The divine power that Paul seeks is not about greed, or revenge, or enviously striving for what another has. Living as a good Christian does not ultimately depend on whether a person measures up according to another Christian but on what God's view of that person is.

Gentleness is thus a gift because it is a means by which God helps us not to worry about what others accomplish—what accolades and awards and, indeed, what human power others might have. If at all possible, then, staying or leaving will have nothing to do with the benefits that a person could get. I am reminded of a Lutheran pastor who eventually joined the Roman Catholic Church. She was a woman and so initially concerned about what it meant to be a woman joining a church where her ordination was no longer recognized. When she finally made a decision for Catholicism, however, her thought was not for any loss of power that she had (divine power or otherwise), but rather that God had shown her that becoming Catholic was just as much her calling as perhaps ordination had been earlier.[2] I am not suggesting that people make decisions against their ordinations because that is a manifestation of power. I am suggesting, however, that if ordination is something that causes one to feel certain of

2. To read this story and similar stories, see Ferrara and Ireland, eds., *The Catholic Mystique.*

one's place in community and against which other things are compared, then perhaps that is a point on which to meditate and discern.

Paul nearly always connects the word *praotēs* with the need to be humble but he also connects it to a need to consider communal concerns. After he has discussed the fruits of the Spirit in ch. 5 of Galatians, Paul mentions gentleness again:

> My friends, if anyone is detected in a transgression, you who have received the Spirit should restore such a one in a spirit of gentleness. Take care that you yourselves are not tempted. Bear one another's burdens, and in this way you will fulfill the law of Christ. For if those who are nothing think they are something, they deceive themselves. All must test their own work; then that work, rather than their neighbor's work, will become a cause for pride. For all must carry their own loads. (Gal 6:1–5)

Paul's explication of gentleness in his letter suggests that the humility of which he speaks is not only one that finds a person not mentioning his own accomplishments, or being sure that he knows "the way." Having the gift of *praotēs* is also a matter of sharing with others in the community—and not only the good things ("Those who are taught the word must share in all good things with their teacher" [Gal 6:6]), but also the things that trouble us. Christians cannot ignore another's problem and say that it is that person's alone to deal with. Or, in the Corinthians' predicament, we would suggest that the people in Apollos's camp are still responsible for bearing with those in Paul's camp and vice versa, even if the group on the other side ends up being "wrong." And moreover, it cannot be an "I told you so" kind of bearing each other up, but must continually be words of humility and, yes, gentleness.

Difficult words to hear, especially in a world that appears to work in exactly opposite ways. Difficult words to hear when even Christian communities—even the earliest Christian communities that we know of—could not easily escape wanting worldly power for themselves. We could imagine this worldly power at work in the Corinthian community: "I'll be on the side for Apollos because it is the side that looks to have the best political advantage." "I'll be on the side for Paul because after all, might makes right." In his writing, though, Paul is able to cut through these false distinctions by showing that there is a different way to view the world. Paul reminds Christians that they do not inhabit a community that is like the world in which we live. At the point where we have set up factions in the way that the world sets up political factions, then here is not a winner or a loser, but a fractured community. The broken community is the one that Paul sees, not a "right side" and a "wrong side."

But this factional need to see a right or wrong side is a terribly sad vision of the world and, additionally, is not very sound ecclesial theology. A view of the church that holds one side as winning seems rather silly in light of a savior whose own "winning" was actually death. As John Howard Yoder has suggested, politics in the Jesus community is far different than politics as it had been imagined before.[3] *The Message* translates "gentleness" as "not needing to force" one's way in life, which might actually be the most apt way to translate what Paul appears to mean. Human power moves tend toward forcing one's own way. Jesus' politics, however, center on not forcing, and yet still being a powerful witness. This shift in viewpoint paves the way for the traditions of Christian martyrdom and Christian pacifism, both ideas that are unthinkable unless one's view of politics has radically changed.

The difficulty, for my students and many others, is in seeing that Jesus' way (and Paul's way) is not a way of doing nothing and shirking duties. It is doing something, but doing it in a way that the world will generally not recognize, which is exactly why we have difficulty seeing it as "something" in the first place. Once the shift in view has been made, it is easy to see that the characteristics of gentleness go far beyond simple passivity, but it will appear passive and likely even weak in the former view. One version of the night hymn known as Tallis Canon (*All Praise to thee, my God, this night*) has a verse that says: "Teach me to live that I may dread the grave as little as my bed. / Teach me to die so that I may rise glorious on that final day." In order to live so as not to dread the grave, one must experience these little deaths. Little deaths are very hard, crushing and bruising to the ego oftentimes—but they do tend to involve this gift of gentleness of not needing to force one's way. And so it seems passive because on my students' view, people ought to be doing everything possible to avoid death, even little deaths of ego, and even more, to help others avoid those little deaths and great deaths too.

When the viewpoint has shifted to Jesus' politics, then, it is also easy to see that not only does gentleness involve humility, and bearing other peoples' burdens in community, but it also involves great courage. The

3. See Yoder, *The Politics of Jesus*.

letter of James uses the word *praotēs* in contrast to evil: "You must under-stand this, my beloved: let everyone be quick to listen, slow to speak, slow to anger; for your anger does not produce God's righteousness. Therefore rid yourselves of all sordidness and rank growth of wickedness, and wel-come with meekness the implanted word that has the power to save your souls" (James 1:19–21). It takes courage, lots of it, to fend against all the evil that is out there, including the evil of estimating yourself higher than others.

Further in Peter's first letter, he says: "Always be ready to make your defense to anyone who demands from you an account of the hope that is in you; yet do it with gentleness and reverence" (1 Pet 3:15b–16). This is not weakness in the sense of doing nothing, for one should be ready to *defend* the faith, just as others defend nations or ideas. But a good defense is not done with weapons of arrogance or feelings that one has the right of way or the power position in a relationship. A good defense is one that does not intentionally provoke. The defender cannot even assume that he is wholly correct, even while he is defending his faith. So yet at the same time, this defense is made by someone who is sure of the faith—but not faith in self, faith in God.

When I think of the stories of people and congregations I know that have left one denomination for another, I think that often gentleness has not been part of their leave-taking. Desire for revenge on someone who has power has been part of those stories. Winning and losing has been part of those stories. To be quite honest, it is part of my story, too. When I was part of the United Methodist Church, I served on national and in-ternational boards and agencies and was on a path toward ordination and even (some said) eventually becoming a bishop. I toyed with the decision to stay or leave for eight years in part because I wanted the power that I had. I liked being able to make top-level decisions and knowing so many people who were bishops and heads of conferences.

I think, too, of the congregations that have left the ELCA or the Presbyterian Church (USA) over the question of women's ordination. Perhaps some of these congregations were gentle in their leaving: that is, prepared to defend their faith but yet to remain in conversation with those with whom they disagreed. With the gift of gentleness, it seems there is ample room for allowing others to be even if there are stark disagree-ments present. I think it is possible both to leave and to display gentleness to the community one has left. But there were many congregations that left that were not gentle to others, at least in the way that Jesus, Paul and James mean.

Sociologists and philosophers argue whether it is possible for altruism to work—whether people can really do things for others without selfishly thinking of themselves first. Along those lines, people might well ask, "Can gentleness be a realistic action? Or is it simply an ideal that we mere humans can never hope to attain?" The gift of gentleness thus seems like a similar case to altruism: asking people to stand down in the face of other peoples' power, or to re-narrate power in new ways, seems more like giving in or giving up, and seems too ideal. It is the same problem that Christian pacifists have: "Your view of reality won't work given what human nature is. People won't stop fighting."

But many Christian pacifists would say that they don't see their task as one of converting people to their "way of thinking" as though Christian pacifism could end war for good or solve all the world's problems. Rather, they see their task as being witnesses to Christ. No matter how improbable the way of gentleness looks, it is not finally about achieving some stated human goal nor even about living as human nature (appears to) intend. Many Christian pacifists readily acknowledge that theirs is not necessarily a path toward world peace. Theirs is instead about giving witness to God, who is not human nor cares about human goals in the same ways we do. So, while a pacifist might hope that doing actions that are alternatives to war might foster a better world, a Christian pacifist does not see that his or her actions will necessarily lead to any human-intended outcome. At the same time, he or she does hope that others will see in their inexplicable actions that God has proclaimed another way—the way of Jesus on the cross.

It is natural to wonder what happened to the communities in Galatia and Corinth. Did they take Paul's advice and calm down? Did they follow the pattern that Christians have seen so often in their own communities and end up splintering into several communities? Did some leave and some stay? Ultimately, it does not matter. What remains of those conversations—what has been deemed worthy of discussion and emulation by countless Christian communities through the centuries—is the Pauline statement that those who live by the Spirit exhibit gentleness. Who cares who won or lost?

So it does not matter who the "winners" and "losers" were then. It seems, too, that to number winners or losers in today's churches would be wrong-headed. What is the right way, whether one stays and especially if one goes, is to witness to Christ in this spirit of gentleness. You have not "won" a fight, you have not "shown them", if you leave. You have not won or lost, likewise, if you stay. In both communities, there might well be people who are elated or dejected that you have left or stayed. But to continue to see the question as an "us versus them" situation is to continue to pit groups together where Christ hoped and prayed there would be no division.

Presbyterian (PCUSA) minister Toby Brown, who writes "A Classical Presbyterian" blog, considers himself one of the dissenters against what he sees as liberal views in the denomination. Brown offers observations about the 2008 General Assembly, where voters approved legislation that removed connections between ordination and sexual conduct.[4] Many observers see that this legislation opens the way for gays, lesbians, bisexuals and transgendered people to be ordained. For Brown, a self-proclaimed evangelical, this has caused some soul searching about what it means to stay in the Presbyterian Church (USA). It would be easy to leave, he knows. He begins a post by saying: "Reformed evangelicals who elect to remain within the PC(USA) at this point now must count the cost and consider their future course. One thing is clear—they will not 'win.'"[5] Brown recognizes, though, that perhaps winning is not the purpose of his work. Instead, in mature reflection, he suggests:

> It's hard enough to keep to one's own path without looking at the steps of others and judging them. Evaluate? Yes. Learn from others? Certainly. Evaluate and take into account missteps and falterings along the way? Of course. But don't let that be so obsessive that one's own path becomes a stumbling block to yourself or others.[6]

He sees that following Christ is his sole purpose, which means the likelihood of staying in a denomination where the majority does not share his theological convictions. To say both that he will not win and yet that he will probably stay takes courage and shows a much different view of gentleness than my students might suppose. He will still look to and

---

4. This amendment and others are still to be voted on by local presbyteries, as of this writing.

5. Toby Brown, "Where from here?"

6. Ibid.

learn from others in his denomination, even those with whom he might disagree.

In the unhappy situation of leaving a church, the best, most *gentle* action is not to participate in one-upmanship, a story of wins and losses. If you are witnessing to the fact that God has called you to this community, and if you acknowledge at the same time that leaving occasions both sadness and joy, then perhaps God has indeed graced you with the gift of gentleness.

Nilus of Sinai, 5th c.

Strive to render your mind deaf and dumb during prayer: then you will be able to pray as you ought.

When you meet with temptation, or are irritated by someone's disagreement, so that you are filled with anger against the one who has disagreed with you, or even say some unseemly word, remember prayer and the judgment (of your conscience before the face of God) during it, and the unseemly movement will at once be stilled in you. Anything you may do to revenge yourself upon a brother who has done you an injustice will offend you during prayer.

Prayer is a branch (of the tree) of meekness, and freedom from anger.

Prayer is an expression of joy and thankfulness.

Prayer is a remedy against sorrow and depression.[1]

---

1. Selection from *Early Fathers from the Philokalia*, 130, §12–16.

5

Kindness

MELISSA MUSICK NUSSBAUM

Where true love and charity are found, God is there.
– Latin office hymn

Clint and Marcia are long time members of the congregation. They raised their children in the church. Clint cleans up after the pancake breakfasts. Marcia brings casseroles for funeral dinners. They have taught Sunday School for over twenty years. Their best friends are fellow church members. When a new pastor arrived, he began getting rid of the old staff. He pointed to the budget deficits. He called the move a staff reduction, a layoff, a cutback. It looked—and felt, to those involved—a lot like a firing. Positions were eliminated. The youth minister's time was halved. She had to leave in order to pay her rent. She joined other staff members who weren't laid off, but whose hours were cut below the minimum necessary for full medical and retirement benefits.

Clint and Marcia were surprised and outraged by the pastor's actions. Neither they nor the congregation learned of the staff reductions until after the fact. They could not understand why they hadn't been given the chance to raise the funds that would allow the church employees to stay on at full time and full salary.

They began to talk of leaving the church, a church they understood to be turning its back on the demand of justice. Those fired had spent, in some cases, decades of their working lives in church offices. And the fired people were more than employees. They were fellow church members, and friends.

Clint and Marcia's talk of leaving the church began to spread. People knew of their commitment to the congregation. They knew that these two would not speak lightly of turning away from the place that had been, for so long, their home. But Marcia said she was finding it increasingly difficult to look at the pastor in the pulpit, or to speak cordially to him in the church halls and meeting rooms. Disagreement over the treatment of church staff was hardening into hatred.

When the pastor convened a congregational meeting to discuss the layoffs, Clint and Marcia were in the front row. After a lengthy explanation of the budget shortfall, the pastor opened the floor to questions. Clint called out "Where's your faith?" He called out again, "You talk like an accountant, not a pastor."

The pastor cautioned Clint about respect. He told him to stop yelling. Then he said that the budget deficit existed "quite apart from his faith or the faith of anyone else, and would have to be addressed. It's not a question of faith, it's a question of money."

Some in the meeting made loud sounds of disgust and disapproval. Clint called the pastor "a fool." The pastor chided him again for his angry tone and manner. The room grew quiet as congregants watched, fearful. If Clint and Marcia left, many knew, others would follow them. The congregation might be wounded in ways that would take years to heal.

Friends persuaded Clint and Marcia to stay. They argued that the heart of the church was with the people and not the pastor. They reminded Clint and Marcia of the births and weddings and funerals they had witnessed together. Clint and Marcia were like family, people said. Leaving the church would destroy the family.

The pastor remained, too, as he would until he received his next assignment. He had no choice in the matter. His way was lonelier, as he had recently replaced a longtime, beloved pastor. Alienated from most of the staff and unknown to most of the church members, he had no confidantes. So he began to talk about the controversy in his sermons, saying how difficult he was finding this first year.

The three of them never came to an agreement about the ways in which the budget deficits were handled. They never agreed on the need to retain or fire staff. They never grew to be friends, or to have any fondness for one another. But, called, as they were, to stay—whether by the demands of the congregation or the demands of ecclesial authorities—neither could the three of them easily avoid or remain separate from one another. Church life brought them together, again and again, day after day, week after week. Thinking of this unhappy trio one can only imagine those Galatians who held differing beliefs on the necessity of circumcision to Christian identity as they met for prayer and teaching, for worship and meals.

What allows Christians to persevere in fellowship when the bonds of natural affection have frayed and broken? What allows Christians to pray and worship together when each believes the other to have betrayed a basic trust? It is another little remarked fruit of the Spirit, kindness, which makes their life in common possible.

Kindness, or *chesed*, is one of the names, or attributes, of God. Kindness is who God is. When Moses goes up to Mount Sinai with the second set of stone tablets he has cut, tablets on which will be written the commandments, he encounters God.

> Having come down in a cloud, the Lord stood there and proclaimed his name, "Lord." Thus the Lord passed before him and cried out, "The Lord, the Lord, a merciful and gracious God, slow to anger and rich in kindness and fidelity. (Exod 34:5–6)

We think of kindness as reciprocal, a sort of societal give and take, a minuet of manners. I say, "Thank you." You respond, "You're welcome." But the kindness that is God has never found reciprocity with Israel nor the Church. We answer God's act of creation with a rebellion. We answer God's creation of family with the murder of one brother at the hands of another. We answer God's incarnation with crucifixion. And so kindness has been defined as an act that has no cause.

There is no cause for God to create the heavens and the earth, no cause to create animals, no cause to create humankind. And there is certainly no cause for God to keep going back to men and women offering forgiveness and mercy each time they turn from him, each time they turn to killing and idolatry.

We are concerned with causes, causes and results. I have heard insanity defined as "Doing the same thing over and over and expecting a different result." There are those who might say that a God who takes Israel back after the Fall, after the days of Noah or after the worship of the golden calf in the wilderness is insane. There are those who would argue that a God who takes human flesh knowing it will be scourged and beaten and hung to die is insane. Insane, meaning a God who does the same thing again and again, each time expecting a different result.

In a homily written for the second Sunday of Lent, Father James T. Burtchaell writes of the first-century Jewish hope for a Messiah who would overthrow Roman oppressors. He describes despair when it appears that Jesus, rather than triumphing, is himself overthrown.

> They [Jesus' disciples] never had realized that Jesus was going to be a strong man, not by what he achieved, not by what he did, not by how he asserted himself, not by how he advanced the cause of a suffering nation, not in how he turned them from a passive people to an energetic and active one. Jesus' great achievements wouldn't be what you and I call achievements. Jesus suffered. He became one more victim to the people who were in power. He became a nothing. They got rid of him . . . It took a good while for it to dawn on them that Jesus had become their Messiah by being a prophet: not by being someone with clout who would retaliate for how they had been struck and afflicted over the years; indeed, not by anything he did, but by what he sustained . . . Jesus' death was the greatest achievement in the history of the world. Jesus, God's only Son, allowed human beings of no account to have their way with him, and he did so, forgiving them. Not just by taking it and being quiet. He actually forgave them as they did it. Jesus' great act was forgiveness of this massive injustice, of perjury, of spite, of jealousy, of brutality.[1]

Jesus acts from the cross. He acts in ways no one could have predicted, or, perhaps, desired. Luke recounts,

> When they came to the place called the Skull, they crucified him and the criminals there, one on his right, the other on his left. Then Jesus said, "Father, forgive them, they know not what they do." (Luke 23:33–34a)

This is kindness, an act with no cause, or—at least—no human cause. Jesus is in the right here; his persecutors in the wrong. He is innocent, and they are guilty. No one faults the innocent man for crying out against his tormentors. No one faults the innocent man for defending himself against

1. Burtchaell, *Collected Homilies*, 1:86.

false charges and punishment. No one faults an innocent man for calling down the full measure of just punishment on his murderers.

Jesus' followers would have cheered had he broken his bounds and killed the soldiers herding him to the cross. They would have raised loud cries of praise if Jesus, like Elijah, had called down heavenly fire to display his heavenly power. And they would have joined him if Jesus, like Elijah, had called out, "Let none of them escape!" before slitting the throats of his tormentors.

Humans want justice—by which we often mean vindication. We want to be declared in the right, and we want the declaration acknowledged. We want our enemies laid low and ourselves raised high. That desire, however well founded, will split a community. If all the parties agree to stay together, then something must take the place of vindication. That something is kindness, *chesed*, for which Burtchaell uses the stark phrase "the refusal to hate." It is a refusal to hate, even when hate is justified, for *chesed* is an act with no cause.

Burtchaell writes:

> Jesus, when he rose from the dead, was never properly understood until they thought back long enough and hard enough, and allowed themselves to see what he had been up to all the time. They finally and reluctantly appreciated that God had done his most spectacular act when that almost unknown man in that far forgotten corner of the world was crucified, and everybody somehow had a hand in it, actively or passively. Yet, when he arose he came to them in love, because he had died in love. He refused to hate.[2]

Hate always has an object, and sometimes it has a justification. Kindness, too, always has an object, but, being of God, it needs no justification. It *is*, as God is. When we practice this fruit of the Spirit we are putting on God, returning good for evil. Acting in kindness, we are acting in kind with God, acting in the style or nature of God. We are acting without human cause, but we are acting in the form, or cause, of God. Human cause demands that we slice off the ear of the arresting soldier in the garden. God restores the ear, healing it and making the man, once again, whole.

By "cause of God," I mean we are acting from the root or foundation of God; we are acting from *who* God is and *how* God is. We are

2. Ibid., 87.

acting, in the simplest and truest sense, as disciples or followers of God. It requires courage and discipline to act in kindness. When we speak of someone "owing me an apology," we mean exactly that: There is a debt and it must be paid. To put aside that debt, to mark it paid when it is not, seems both unsatisfying and wrong. We worry that putting aside a debt will embolden the thief, that returning good for evil will strengthen the hand of the wicked. This is all reasonable, I think, but it is *our* nature, *our* reason, and not God's. Jesus' act of returning good for evil on the cross destroys death, setting in irrevocable motion the unraveling of all that is wicked and wrong.

In his homily Burtchaell speaks of Christians caught up in the ethnic struggles of our time:

> Think of the terrible maelstrom of violence, particularly as it has manifested old hatreds and distrust and grudges between people supposedly because of their different beliefs in God. And think of the people whom we'll never read about or know by name, people who at risk of their own lives would ignore old grudges and protect some helpless neighbors; people who refused to retaliate; people who fought off the hatred; people who had every reason to steal, to kill, to hate, but didn't . . . Their heroic moment may have been when they simply and strenuously refused to hate.[3]

"They simply and strenuously refused to hate." A simple act because the refusal to hate requires neither arms nor money. The refusal to hate doesn't need a strategic geographic advantage or an intricate plan. The refusal to hate needs no funding, no multi-national "coalition of the willing." It needs only a willing heart. But Burtchaell wisely adds the adjective "strenuous" to the adjective "simple," because while simple, the refusal to hate is also simply impossible. We do not act out of our fruits or our gifts we when we act in kindness. Rather, we act out of the fruits or gifts given us by the Holy Spirit. We act out of the abundance of God shared with us in the Spirit.

Notice, too, that kindness does not mean surrender or denial. If Clint and Marcia believe the way church employees are treated is unjust, they must seek justice. If the pastor believes he acted in justice, he must continue to act justly. Both parties are allowed to press their cases, but they must do so with kindness. Pressing one's case with kindness will also

---

3. Ibid., 86–87.

demand that one examine the case in light of other's objections. Debate? Yes, and strenuous advocacy. They must simply and strenuously refuse to hate.

Paul writes near the end of his letter to the Galatians,

> Brothers, even if a person is caught in some transgression, you who are spiritual should correct that one in a gentle spirit, looking to yourself, so that you also may not be tempted. Bear one another's burdens, and so you will fulfill the Law of Christ. (Gal 6:1–2)

Paul's "gentle spirit" is another way to speak of kindness. He commands us to look upon one another with a gentle spirit because any honest self-examination—"look to yourself"—will reveal our own transgressions. We, who call upon, who cling to, God's unwarranted kindness, are called to offer it to our brothers and sisters. Paul is clear about the nature of the transgressions within the Galatian church. Those transgressions do not overcome the need for members of the Body to show God's kindness, God's *chesed*, to one another.

Interior Castles

TERESA OF AVILA

Not long ago a very learned man told me that souls who do not practice prayer are like people with paralyzed or crippled bodies; even though they have hands and feet they cannot give orders to these hands and feet. Thus there are souls so ill and so accustomed to being involved in external matters that there is no remedy, nor does it seem they can enter within themselves. They are now so used to dealing always with the insects and vermin that are in the wall surrounding the castle that they have become almost like them. And though they have so rich a nature and the power to converse with none other than God, there is no remedy. If these souls do not strive to understand and cure their great misery, they will be changed into statues of salt, unable to turn their heads to look at themselves, just as Lot's wife was changed for having turned her head.[1]

1. Teresa of Avila, *The Interior Castle*, 38.

6

Goodness

JANA MARGUERITE BENNETT

Thy mercies never shall remove; Thy nature and Thy name is Love.
– Charles Wesley

Any discussion of goodness for Christians surely cannot take place without considering Jesus' statement to the rich ruler: "Why do you call me good? No one is good but God alone" (Luke 18:19). It's a complex passage, not the least because Christians have held that Jesus is the incarnate Son, the second person of the Trinity, and therefore is God. Even without this theological conundrum, though, there is a stark question to be asked. If even Jesus sees that he cannot call himself good, then where do we mere humans stand? The statement implies that humans cannot be or do good in themselves—even decisions we make cannot be counted as good just at our say so. We like to think, for instance, that we are being good when, say, we give money to a homeless person on the street. Yet there are so many points to consider that might make that action not so good: we might (even unknowingly) be giving money as a matter of pride—"Look how good I am." We might be handing money to someone who only seems homeless to us, and who is therefore insulted. We might be giving money to someone who didn't need money so much as a ride somewhere or a hot meal. The gift we want to give might not have turned out to be a good gift.

We can be so easily deceived about what is the "good thing" that counting on ourselves alone to make that determination is sketchy, at best.

This is why goodness is rightly counted as a gift from God and not as something that we humans can manufacture or determine. We do not know what it is to be good, yet we have been given ways in which to think about and begin to understand goodness. Jesus' statement gives a description of who God is, which is "good." Goodness is God's own activity and essence.

If God alone is good, there is no goodness inherently in us and no action we can make that would make us be good (be God). Yet in orthodox theology, the mystery of the Trinity is that God has invited us to participate in God's own life anyway, and through that life we do have some inkling of what good is. God created us in the *imago dei*, the image of God, and so we can be the image of some of that good. God has also revealed the Triune life to us through Jesus Christ, and that revelation gives us an inkling of that good.

Thus, we know good things by analogy to the One Good. The three-year-old desires chocolate cookies because they taste good; the teenager wants the newest video game because it makes him feel good; the adult looks for a reliable car or a large house because they encompass the "good life." The little things, and even creation as a whole, are not inherently good on their own, but only because God has created them and gifted them with some sense of goodness.

God has created us with desire, which turns out to be related to goodness. The thirteenth-century theologian Thomas Aquinas suggests that desire is for good.[1] Every human action tends toward goodness, even if it is merely something that seems good and is not actually good. For example, stealing something can, to the thief, seem to be good because he gets something that he wants. What the thief does not recognize is that in terms analogously to God's own life, his activity is not good.

We are like that thief, more often that we want to admit. In our actions, we do want to do something well but what we are not able to admit to ourselves often enough is that even our own sense of goodness fails. And that is one of the scariest parts about discerning whether to stay in a congregation or leave.

---

1. *Summa contra gentiles* 1:306–7.

The thief's difficulty in knowing what is good becomes all the more clear when we look at our culture's sense of goodness. It is no wonder that any of us should ask the question of whether we are making the right or good decision. Ours is a particularly unforgiving culture when it comes to things that we deem good or not.

Think of all the things that make for the good life for us Americans: We must have the perfect, sexy career, and going to college is deemed pretty much necessary to get that perfect law, or medical, or political career. Trades, despite paying more, are not the good jobs—parents want their children in medical school or law school if at all possible. We must have the perfect number of children at the correct time. Having sex once that results in a pregnancy (especially for a teenage girl, but also for a career woman, or a woman with more than the socially acceptable number of children) seems to be a mistake of catastrophic proportions. Not only should those children be born at the perfect time but they need to be perfect: they need to win, to be geniuses even at the age of three months. They need to be perfect so they can show the world their parents are perfect, too.

In this culture, our bodies must be perfect too. Acne creams and moisturizers precede wrinkle creams and more moisturizers. People with money get plastic surgery to tighten up those areas that seem unsightly or inject poison into their wrinkles to smooth them over. Dieting remains a big deal and an even bigger business, so that we chase after the ever elusive ideal of looking like the magazine supermodel, forgetting that *her* perfection was airbrushed in. Houses, cars, clothes . . . all of it has the good ideal we must live up to, especially in our era of green living. It must have the Energy Star label and be made of recycled tires or, even better, recycled plastic bags.

Even the mundane aspects of our lives have been touched by this perfectionism. Eating is one example. Food must be perfectly manufactured to include the precise amount of vitamins and minerals that a scientist deems to be most helpful for our bodies. Eggs are now formulated (well the chicken feed is, anyway) to contain DHA—the necessary Omega-3 fatty acid for brain function and creating healthy bodies. Far more troubling is a recent survey done by the University of North Carolina that suggests at least sixty-five percent of all women have some sort of disordered unhealthy eating pattern (skipping meals, avoiding even "good" carbohydrates, etc.), stemming from cultural obsession with dieting. This doesn't count the additional ten percent who have the more notorious eating disorders of anorexia, bulimia, and similar diseases.[2]

The obvious answer, from a Christian point of view, is simply to resist those things that society deems to be good but which are clearly "bad" on Christian terms. We think, perhaps there are places in Scripture that might tell us about eating better or that might help us resist the "perfect children" ideal. Scripture may not be as helpful as we wish, however, for perhaps on other points, as with energy-saving devices, we could find in Scripture support for that ideal. The distinction between what seems good culturally but bad on Christian terms is easier to make when the decision is between trying to amass as much wealth as possible for one's own fun, and using that money to feed the poor; it is much less easy when the perfection we try to manufacture is one that is mandated in Scripture, like being good stewards of the earth.

Discernment between culture and Christian values is often not that apparent. Is it more Christian to buy a new house that has been fitted with all the latest environmentally-sound gadgets so that one is saving the earth? Or is it better to make do and buy an older house so that one is not using more of the earth's resources in building? Or would it even be far better not to buy a house at all?

So, in a culture where flitting from brand to brand, shopping for the most perfect item that fits the perfect ideals, it is difficult to discern the goodness, or not, of switching from church to church. In this book, we have not been in favor of church shopping and of succumbing to the consumer mentality of "finding the perfect church" as though congregations were like toothpaste (toothpaste with whitener for brown teeth, but toothpaste with whitener and tartar control for teeth that happen to require both, each product being appropriate for each individual's teeth).

Still, when Paul suggests that goodness is one of the fruits of the Spirit and our notions of goodness are so formed by the views of perfection, it would seem that of course, there must be the "good" church out there that will make me "good" and that will present the best decision possible. So, it is no surprise that people should ask whether they are making good decisions when it comes to staying in or leaving a congregation. In a culture of perfection, being judged for imperfection is hellish. It is difficult to know what the good act is when the purported good things extol perfection to

---

2. "65% of women in U.S. have eating disorders," *Women's Health News.*

such a degree that it becomes a vice. Goodness—one of the greatest gifts the Spirit could endow on someone in our culture—is yet probably one of the most difficult to discern, because of the competing varieties of what counts as "good."

So, how *would* a person know whether she was making a good decision or determine whether she failed? I often ask my students how they might know whether something is good or not. They usually first suggest that feeling bad about a result of a decision indicates that it was a poor decision to make. Therefore, if that result might occur and would make you feel bad, that is not the right decision. This kind of reasoning, however, puts the burden of proof on one's emotions and it is not at all clear that one's emotions adequately describe the results of a decision. In a few months, my husband and I are moving to another state. It was a difficult decision to make and there are many times when we feel upset about leaving our present situation. On the other hand, we know that our decision is a good one for us—the emotions go along with the simple fact that we are leaving people we know and love. If decisions were grounded in whether they make us feel okay or not, we might never make them, because oftentimes the decision to be made is between two mediocre options.

Determining the goodness of a decision also cannot be grounded in knowing that the action itself is good. This is already apparent from the fact that people invest time and considerable discernment into whether to leave or stay. If one or the other action were transparently good, it would be obvious what the choice should be, even if one chose not to do that good act. Thinking of Paul's Galatian community gives another example: the people ask, "Circumcised or uncircumcised?" Paul refuses to dichotomize the question in that way and even suggests to the people that it is a bad question to begin with. Neither one state or the other is sufficient enough to be called "good" from Paul's point of view. In fact, harping on one's state is decidedly not good.

Even one's good intentions cannot be sufficient for calling a decision "good". That someone *means* for an act to be good does not make it good. Well-meaning friends might set a person up with a blind date but even if that person knows they intended something good in that act, it doesn't make the result, the blind date, good. When considering leaving or staying in a church, the intentions are even more difficult to discern. The intentions require that one know the story of the person's journey and not generalize a specific case.

The philosopher Elizabeth Anscombe suggests that intention cannot be separated from the action itself.[3] There is no separate mental realm in which I work out my intentions and then, knowing my intentions, act. My intentions become apparent as I act so that the action and the intention are wrapped up together. I may be aware of what some of my intentions but at the same time, it is possible to be deceitful about intentions or to be deceived by someone else's.

People have further suggested that a decision can be deemed good if the place or the time is "right." A couple may decide to get married, for instance, but if the two people are twelve years old at the time, we will be likely to say that marriage is a bad decision. Time and place come into the question of goodness but are not ultimate determining factors for good-ness, in themselves. For example, those twelve-year-olds to be married could reside in a culture where it is perfectly acceptable to be married at the age; in that culture, the timing is right. The age, twelve, is not a simple litmus test for determining the goodness of that marriage.

All of these—time and place, intention, the relative goodness of leav-ing or staying—do tell something about whether a decision is the good one, but at the same time, these are not sufficient.

Goodness is a great unknown. The person who asks, "Am I doing the right thing?" is asking exactly the right question, but exactly the wrong question too. The question itself is unanswerable—we cannot know if it is good at this exact moment. As I suggested above, part of the difficulty with the question is that we do not have a clear way to determine how we might go about assessing the goodness of the decision. Goodness is not determined by feeling, circumstance, or willingness. It is not even clear when we *might* know that it was a good decision. Tomorrow or next month? Ten years from now? The unanswerability makes the question exactly the right one because it pinpoints the mystery of the life that Christians are called to live because we are mysteriously called into God's own life. We cannot fathom God and so we cannot fathom what it might mean to be all good—to make the absolutely good decision.

Yet I know that this conclusion of mine will be quite unsatisfactory. If Paul suggested to the Galatians that goodness was one of the fruits of the Spirit, surely there is a way to discern that goodness even though that goodness ultimately belongs to God alone. If the Spirit has given it, it must

---

3. Anscombe, *Intention*.

be there. But it is for this reason that the question "Am I doing the right thing?" is exactly the wrong one to ask. Maybe the questions are, instead, "Do I have enough reason to believe God is leading me somewhere else?" and "Is the community of which I am part forming me well?"

The gift of goodness makes clear that any goodness we might have is truly a gift—we cannot manufacture it or will it to come. Even if we think we are good, we must get rid of those notions. For how can any act I do, no matter how good I think it is, compare to the knowledge of God as good?

We must learn to share in God's goodness. God invites us to share in God's life, particularly through prayer. Despite the failed senses of what goodness means, still there is the invitation to call God "Father" and to be in the kind of intimate relationship with God that Jesus shows, as the Son. One thing we know from the Gospels is how often Jesus is in prayer, and how Jesus says that he is the "way" to God—that no one can come to the Father except through him.

How, too, are we to understand goodness any better unless to ask the source of goodness, God? Prayer involving silence, listening, and contemplation becomes of utmost importance if we are to receive the gift of goodness. Personal prayer, then, continues to be a necessity for the person seeking whether to stay or leave.

Yet personal prayer can be deceitful, just like the thief who thinks he is desiring good things but is cultivating bad things. We can be telling ourselves lies when we think we are praying and then it is necessary to turn to the places and people who first taught us to pray in the first place. Jesus calls us into fellowship with each other, to be members of his Body. Corporate worship is as necessary as personal prayer. Corporate worship is likely to be the most difficult prayer to participate in when one struggles with whether to leave or stay. This prayer, though, is a most intimate participation in God's own life and has great potential for showing us goodness.

Prayer is one antidote to the culture of perfection. Another is willingness to seek forgiveness—to admit the possibility that the decision may be wrong, even at the time of making it. In an era where nearly everything we do comes with some standard of perfection that can be measured (waistline, energy output, presence of Omega 3 fatty acids), Christians learn to forgive each other and to accept that perfection will not be there. Perfection will not be in the congregation one leaves nor in the congregation one finds a home in. People will, indeed, be upset when someone leaves their fold. Others might well be upset to find that "she" is now a member of this congregation. Forgiving each others' failings is one act that leads us closer to God despite the fact that we cannot be all good in the way that the God toward which we stumble is good. "Forgive us our sins as we forgive those who sin against us."

In addition, the antidote to an obsession with perfection is to broaden the perspective of the decision. When it comes to having the gift of goodness in staying or leaving, what comes to mind is that the act of leaving or staying is not itself a good action, as though it were divorced from other actions, or indeed, separated from a whole host of actions that a person might make. While it seems that The Decision—that is, the choice about whether to stay where you are or become part of another Christian group—seems to be the doorway on which everything else hinges, it is important not to ignore all the other facets going into that one decision. Making a decision to stay is accompanied by lots of other, seemingly smaller actions, choices, decisions: committing to be on a church committee or teach Sunday School or be lector are all activities that contribute to keeping a person involved in the community. On the flip side, showing up sporadically, or missing meetings, or attending another parish are actions that are on the way toward leaving a congregation. Prayer, participation in the lives of specific congregations, and study of theology are important ways of participating in God's own good life.

Consider Michael Westmoreland-White's move from the Southern Baptist Convention toward the Alliance of Baptists. Westmoreland-White is a Baptist theologian and blogger who writes of his own journey that involves conversion to Christianity, as well as "conversion" from one Christian denomination to another. From one point of view, he could seem like a church shopper searching for the church that fits his own personal theology. He writes in one blog entry:

> I found that the institutions of the SBC were being taken over by those who stressed inerrancy . . . , were hostile to critical biblical studies, opposed male-female equality and the ordination of women, and were mostly aligned with conservative Republican politics. Later, opposition to legal abortions (with which I had some sympathy) and to either equal inclusion of GLBT [Gay, Lesbian,

Bisexual, Transgendered] folk in church life or civil liberties for GLBT folk would be added.[4]

Yet to understand Westmoreland-White's action in moving from the Southern Baptist Convention to the Alliance of Baptists, it is necessary to consider his entire story. He converted to Christianity from self-proclaimed agnosticism through some African American Baptist friends. Before he could be baptized and join a Baptist congregation in the U.S., however, he joined the Army and found himself in Germany. The German Baptists he encountered were pacifists who deeply shaped his own pacifism even while in the Army.

When he returned to the U.S., he quickly joined a Southern Baptist congregation, not knowing that there were differences among Baptists. He soon discovered that, unlike the German Baptists who are largely pacifist, there are few pacifists among the Southern Baptists. But moreover, he began seminary studies right around the time that the Southern Baptist Convention began pushing for certain doctrinal commitments like the inerrancy of Scripture. He suggests that these theological disagreements would not in themselves have led to moving to the Alliance of Baptists. Yet the experiences he had had with African-American and German Baptists were so disparate compared to his experiences in the Southern Baptist Convention that it led to further historical and theological study of what it means to be baptist.[5]

Through his studies, he gained an appreciation of the broader baptist tradition (including Anabaptists) and concludes: "I am a Baptist as part of the larger Believers Church tradition, that collection of denominational groups which *always* rejects legal establishment, which must be joined individually by personal faith and believers' baptism, and which stresses active discipleship and gathered churches of visible saints."[6] I think Westmoreland-White's questions and studies are not finally about himself and his own rightness in making a decision. His reflections were instead about tradition, what makes for a Baptist community, and whether God wanted him to be formed by that community.

---

4. Westmoreland-White, "Encounters with Tradition."

5. Westmoreland-White uses the lowercase "b" intentionally to refer to baptists across the globe.

6. Westmoreland-White, "Encounters with Tradition."

Actions that lead us toward or away from a Christian community should be accompanied with the totality of living a Christian life. Prayer, fasting, reading Scripture, study of theology, perfectly or not, are all part of that life. The Spirit's gift of goodness will not be received in this decision to stay or go unless we participate in the life God has shown in the first place.

The Way of the Pilgrim

He opened the book, found the instruction by St. Simeon the New Theologian and read: "Sit down alone and in silence. Lower your head, shut your eyes, breathe out gently and imagine yourself looking into your own heart. Carry your mind, i.e., your thoughts, from your head to your heart. As you breathe out, say 'Lord Jesus Christ, have mercy on me.' Say it moving your lips gently, or simply say it in your mind. Try to put all other thoughts aside. Be calm, be patient, and repeat the process very frequently."

He turned to the teaching of Nicephorus and read, "'If after a few attempts you do not succeed in reaching the realm of your heart in the way you have been taught, do what I am about to say, and by God's help you will find what you seek. The faculty of pronouncing words lies in the throat. Reject all other thoughts (you can do this if you will) and allow that faculty to repeat only the following words constantly, 'Lord Jesus Christ, have mercy on me.' Compel yourself to do it always. If you succeed for a time, then without a doubt your heart will open to prayer. We know it from experience."[1]

1. *The Way of the Pilgrim*, 9–11.

7

Patience
JANA MARGUERITE BENNETT

Keep Thou my feet; I do not ask to see
The distant scene—one step enough for me

– John Henry Newman

I suspect that for most people, patience is not a gift—God-given or otherwise. Patience involves waiting, going slowly, deliberating, doing one thing at a time, being long-suffering, enduring. Ours is not a culture that privileges that kind of taking time. We think highly of efficiency, and we value the ability to multi-task. Fast food, rather than the food that requires patience to plan, shop for, chop, mix and cook, is a mainstay for people moving from one life-enhancing activity (a job) to another (an extracurricular pursuit). Being able to communicate by cell phone, email, and text messaging allows us to ask questions and receive answers and to touch base with family and friends, even across the globe, in a matter of seconds. The fast and efficient life can involve a great many more (generally good) activities than it otherwise would if we had to wait for food to be prepared (or prepare food ourselves) or if we had to wait for handwritten letters of permission to arrive and the like. In this context, patience is most definitely not a virtue, let alone a gift.

Patience is antithetical to efficiency and the most money earned/ stocks sold/cows butchered in the shortest amount of time. Time is money, so they say, and the drive for efficiency relates to that knowledge. History textbooks that describe the move from cottage industries to the industrial revolution and machine-made goods do so from the perspective that one cottar and his wife sewing shoes could not make nearly the money for their business or someone else's as a machine could. Profits were there for the taking so long as people recognized the value of efficiency. And where the value of efficiency is recognized, the value of patience cannot be.

But it is not only efficiency that we have to contend with when it comes to viewing patience as a gift or as a virtue. David Bailey Harned suggests that we also see a connection (or more pointedly, a disconnection) between patience and justice.[1] To do justice means often to act quickly. If one hears of a child abuse case, for example, speed rather than slow deliberateness is seen as the more virtuous activity, and likewise with other forms of violence. Patience seems to ignore real problems and the plights of suffering people, while a certain righteous impatience affirms solidarity and compassion with and for the poor and those in trouble.

Justice and efficiency seem to win out against patience in modern society. In the context of considering leaving one Christian community for another, patience is likewise often not a gift, particularly where the disconnection between justice and patience exists. Entire congregations have left communions and denominations over matters that are deemed "matters of justice" and this kind of leaving affects both so-called liberal and conservative groups. In the current Christian arguments about homosexuality, for example, conservative groups have discerned a need to leave the Episcopalian communion in America because the communion condones ordination of gays and lesbians, while liberal congregations in the United Methodist Church have seen the need to break away in the face of votes against ordination of gays. There is a history of this kind of leaving, too. Groups that split from congregations over racial tensions in the pre-and post-Civil War era had significant concerns about justice and particularly about their ability to be Christian in a church that would not acknowledge them as full Christians.

Neither homosexuality nor race relations are often seen as matters of Christian doctrine but more as matters of "social justice," (which does a disservice to questions surrounding homosexuality and race relations because so-called social justice questions are matters of theology;

1. Harned, *Patience*, 2.

rightly thinking and speaking about God). Nonetheless, there have also been times when matters of what might be considered systematic theological doctrine have also been considered matters of justice. The Eastern Orthodox Church and the Roman Catholic Church, for example, split over the doctrinal question of authority, and that was a matter of justice in the most traditional sense: what is owed to whom? Does the Bishop of Rome have the authority to request allegiance over such things as a change in the Nicene Creed (the filioque clause) or the ways in which liturgy is practiced? If he is seen as having Peter's Seat, then he does have that authority, and injustice is done in not following him. But if not, or if his authority is seen in a different configuration as the Orthodox believe, then injustice is done in obeying the Pope's orders.

I have been speaking of congregations here, but the individual who leaves one parish for another may also be leaving for reasons of justice: matters of abuse and neglect, or matters of doctrine. In all these examples, it is a question of whose justice is being considered and to whom allegiance is owed. On one hand, justice is owed to those who are suffering; on the other hand, isn't loyalty to a specific group of people (particularly a group that has baptized and raised you in faith) a matter of justice? (And don't they suffer, as well?) Deciding to leave or stay on these terms becomes a particularly agonizing decision because it seems that an impossible choice is given: either one is siding with "justice" or one is siding with loyalty to a congregation and thus, apparently, to acting patiently in one's life with that congregation. A person's patience seemingly becomes about persisting with the people in that congregation, no matter what the circumstances, until (perhaps) the day comes when the demands for justice simply outweigh all other considerations and the person, or congregation, is compelled to leave. The choice the potential convert has seems clear. He either accepts a given situation and waits patiently with that congregation, or he chooses to leave. The choice seems to be about measuring when one has been "patient enough" and when one has not, assuming a person concedes that patience is even necessary.

Yet perhaps that is not the choice that must be made. Is our discernment about staying or leaving really about a patience or justice dichotomy? When might it be possible to say that we should act quickly (apparently without patience) and when is it better to patiently endure? When, in other words, is patience a gift that is manifested in us?

Scriptural witness questions some of the assumptions we might make about patience. Consider Anna and Simeon in the second chapter of Luke, for example, who had been waiting a lifetime for the child they knew would be here some day. Their patience mirrored the patience of their people: a Messiah would some day come because God had promised it. Anna and Simeon would not necessarily see that day come any more than any of the hundreds of other waiting people would see that day. But their waiting is connected to a different sense of justice. There were many instances that might be considered injustice that the Hebrew people had to face in the 400 years or so between the prophecies about a Messiah and the actual appearance of the Messiah: the Babylonian exile, in which people were forcibly marched across desert to live in a foreign city; the colonization of Hebrew lands by Hellenized peoples whose power was so great that the entire language and culture changed;[2] the governance of Israel by Roman authorities, who tolerated Judaism but who also imposed their own high priests and eventually sought to impose the Cult of the Emperor as well.[3] Despite these injustices, Anna and Simeon still kept their watch, believing that eventually God would act to correct them. The implication of the passage is that Anna and Simeon are blessed to see the Christ in part because they have been waiting patiently on God's action.

Some might argue, however, that waiting on God is a far different thing than having patience with our human Christian communities. After all, we know that God works in God's own time, but in between all of that, humans are supposed to be doing *something*. So, Anna and Simeon waited, but the Maccabees revolted against their oppressors and person after person in Galilee rose to try to restore the Israelite kingdom. There was activity happening, in addition to the waiting. Perhaps the biblical witness is to say that patience does not negate revolutionary action.

The biblical witness complicates this view of things, however, in the story of Jonah. In the fourth chapter of Jonah, God has just forgiven the people of Ninevah for their crimes because they have repented. Seeing this, Jonah says to God: "O Lord! Is this not what I said while I was still in my own country? That is why I fled to Tarshish at the beginning; for I knew that you are a gracious God and merciful, slow to anger, and abounding in steadfast love, and ready to relent from punishing. And now, O Lord,

2. Roetzel, *The World that Shaped the New Testament*, 11.

3. Ibid., 16–17.

please take my life from me, for it is better for me to die than to live" (Jonah 4:2–4). And the Lord said, "Is it right for you to be angry?" The key here is to know that Ninevah is a Babylonian city, of the very people who exiled the kingdom of Judah by forcing its people to march across the desert to exile. The contrast between Jonah's understandable anger at the people who so badly mistreated his own people, and God's steadfast love shows clearly. God is a God of patience, open to the possibility that even the people of Ninevah might repent of their sins and follow God. But God's patience is just as perplexing to Jonah as it might be to us today. Doesn't God care about the injustices done to the Hebrews? Why should God reward those who have committed crimes, particularly against God's own people?

Jonah knows regardless of what he thinks about the matter, God will be God. Jonah might try to escape from God's own nature by getting on a boat and sailing to Tarshish but ultimately, Jonah's own power does not stand in the face of God's nature to be patient. Jonah's own actions of trying to get out from under God's rather oppressive (from his point of view) steadfast love cannot win. God is always identified as the one who holds the ultimate power, and God's power appears to be the power of patience. God would rather forgive those people who commit crimes even if it takes years and even when it looks as though repentance will never happen. God's sense of justice stands in contrast to Jonah's sense of justice, and the contrast manifests in Jonah's anger. But God has further lessons to give Jonah about justice and patience: God causes a vine to grow to provide shade for Jonah, but then demolishes the vine the next day. Jonah expresses anger at this injustice, so much so that he wishes he were dead. God, however, uses this example as an analogy between the vine and the city of Ninevah; as Jonah cares about the vine, so God cares about Ninevah and all its inhabitants.

Jonah's witness for us is to suggest even our actions will be ultimately futile in the face of God's own activity. Patience, then, does seem like inactivity. Patience becomes discounted as "doing nothing," a synonym for indifference and passivity. Today we err on the side of impatience largely, I suspect, because of our sense of the need for justice. I imagine that those who disagree with what I write in this essay will do so by way of example: what about the woman in an abusive and life-threatening relationship? Surely she should not be patient in her zeal to get out of that relationship. This is very likely true (though I could conceive of circumstances where a bit of patience—planning a good time to leave, stashing some money somewhere—might possibly be good). The point in this example is probably not the woman in the abusive relationship, however, but the friend who has cared enough to point this out as an example. The friend feels helpless in this situation—wants desperately to get the woman away from the abusive spouse and finds that she/he cannot. If the friend tries to force the issue, often the victim returns to the abuser anyway. It is the extraordinary patience of the friend that ought to be the focus. Which is not to say that the friend should do nothing: patience is not about doing nothing because waiting could still involve activity such as giving the woman the numbers to the domestic abuse hotline. Patience cannot be forced on someone else.

At the end of it all, there will always be those situations against which we feel helpless and where the main thing to do is to wait. Might there be a way in which patience does not imply passivity? Can it be the case that patience is itself an *activity* that must be acknowledged as a good and potentially faithful act given the context? Patience is communal: it seeks to include many people, those who are quick and those who are not. Just as God showed Jonah the divine care that included concern for even the Babylonians, so Christians might recognize that patience allows for consideration of people who might otherwise be lost in the shuffle: children, elderly, the poor, and even, in the case of Jonah, one's enemies. The activity of patience is the activity, in part, of waiting for these people because that is, in fact, justice.

In this sense, patience is an offensive action, to use football terminology. Patience is no defensive activity that we do in response to someone else's ill-intentioned actions, or against moves designed to foil our own attempts to live a Christian life. It is rather an activity that we do out of a sense of necessity for our own well-being. We need it to live life rightly and to interact with others well. Passivity, by contrast, is a defensive mechanism, I suspect. It is borne out of a sense that one cannot "change anything" because nothing's ever changed before, so why bother? To an outsider, a person could appear either patient or passive and it could look very similar.

However, the theologian W. H. Vanstone suggests that "*any* sort of waiting presupposes some kind or degree of *caring*."[4] If one does not care,

---

4. Vanstone, *The Stature of Waiting*, 102.

one does not bother to wait for the older woman who walks slowly and stiffly, for others whose points of view seem 'archaic,' for the child who has not yet learned how to ask for what he wants. To care for these people is to wait, and hopefully, to want to wait. Vanstone continues by suggesting that the person who does not deem very many things to be important will be a very impatient person. Or put in a different light, the things that we consider "worth waiting for" demonstrate very much the kind of people we are. We do tend to care more for the people and things that we have awaited. The expensive toy that took months to save up to buy tends to have a special place on the shelf and in memory.

Waiting is a kind of gracious act and gift to those who are waited upon. It implies due consideration of all the people concerned, and is not therefore an act in which a solely self-interested person can engage. Patience requires paying attention to another person (an elderly relative) or to a process (farming). People who are clearly dependents show the need for patience most obviously, though if we are perceptive, we begin to realize that we too, however able-bodied or mature we are, are also dependent and need for people to wait on us. If we are truly perceptive, we begin to see all the ways in which patience is actually alive (if not quite well) in our world, despite the fast food and the instantaneous communication: the people who do foster care, the family members waiting patiently as their loved ones struggle with terminal illness.

Thus, part of realizing whether the gift of patience is manifest in discernment about staying or leaving is considering the extent to which one pays attention to those who are dependent. In this view, patience is itself a matter of justice and not a denial of justice. But it is a conception of justice that involves as many people as possible. The most difficult part of this point is realizing that we are all dependents of each other when it comes to Christian community. In Paul's famous analogy, the members of the Body are dependent on the others so that the hand should not hope to be an eye. Rational adults are not dependent on each other in the same way that children and the very sick are dependent, but still, we depend on each other at least to be present on Sunday morning. We depend on the fact that someone in the congregation will be doing the morning's scripture readings and someone will be there to do the ushering. Even if we ourselves *could* do that activity, we are still dependent on the others who do.

Waiting can be a gift to ourselves even as it is a gift to others. In most cases, I suspect, the decision one is making to leave or stay in a church is not at all like that of the woman with the abusive husband. I think of a couple I know, Brad and Kelly, who belonged to a small evangelical congregation they liked very much. After being members there for some years, they found themselves in the midst of congregational upheaval over a new program their pastor was introducing. More and more members started leaving because they disagreed with pastor's unequivocal decision to buy a very expensive program that most of them felt was not theologically astute enough. Soon, a financial crisis loomed too, due to the loss in membership. Brad and Kelly also disagreed with the pastor's new program but weren't quite sure they wanted to make the jump to another congregation. Besides, they asked, where would we go? So many of their friends who had left, left altogether and did not join a new church. They did not want to take that step, especially as they had three small children they wanted to raise in a good congregation. They had simply hoped that the congregation of which they were part would be that congregation in which to raise their children. In the midst of the theological and financial upheaval in the church, Brad and Kelly decided to wait and be patient. After four years of prayer and reading books and discerning with each other, they did decide to leave for another church. For them, I think the patience was important: it enabled them to move away from the knee-jerk reactions that many in the parish had to thoughtfully reading and discussing their pastor's program. They gave it a chance, but not without also doing a great deal of reflection. Moreover, Brad and Kelly's patience enabled them to know, at the end of their period of discernment, which church they now wanted to join.

Practicing patience allows us not to be constrained by contemporary notions of time and needing to get things done quickly, including such significant moves as leaving one community for another. If someone is even asking a question like "when is the point when I have been patient enough with these people," the very fact of that question implies impatience. Impatience implies a lack of hope that something good might come of a situation, and from the Christian point of view, there should always be hope that another person could experience a real conversion. That, too, implies a sense of justice—justice accorded to the one who would otherwise be dismissed as someone "who will never change". It seems that the questions one is asking ought to have changed if one is truly being "patient enough."

The practice of patience is thus a bit like the practice of Sabbath. Sabbath is one day a week when people proclaim, "I am not a person who was made to work." The day is spent reveling in God and in play, because it is the day that God delighted in his own creation. When we practice Sabbath, we learn to delight as well. On the Sabbath there is nothing to prove—either to one's self or to others. I once practiced Sabbath with some juniors and seniors in high school who were thinking about Christian practices and what it means to live them. This group of teenagers determined that playing soccer, just for the pure joy of it, was an acceptable Sabbath practice, but if that game veered into competitiveness, the joy of the game itself was taken away. But to learn to enjoy something—not for its usefulness, but simply for the pure fun of it—took some time. It was an odd experience for my teenagers because it was so contrary to much of what they had been told or had gotten used to. Practicing patience is, in some sense, a Sabbath.

The recent crisis in the Episcopalian Church in relation to the Anglican world communion ought to raise questions for everyone, Anglican or not, about patience. Philip Turner suggests that the issues that have come to the forefront in the ECUSA are part and parcel of what it has meant to be a modern person and an American. We are in love with the idea of the autonomous individual and with the idea that a person's identity is more wrapped up in notions of rights and individual characteristics than in a community. What would it mean, instead, to see justice as a matter of the entire community? How would conservative African bishops need to respond to their gay and lesbian brothers and sisters? How, in turn, would gays and lesbians and their supporters need to respond to their African brothers and sisters? Is leaving, for either group, the only way to resolve questions of justice? (And, I would add, there are several questions of justice here: justice for gays and lesbians is the one most noted by North Americans, but there is also consideration of what justice means for those in parts of Africa for whom a pro-vote on homosexuality is equivalent to a death sentence, among other things. And finally, there is, I think, a larger question of justice for the worldwide communion as a whole, and related questions about justice toward God.)

While God is one who seeks justice, God is also a patient God. The apparent disconnection between patience and justice falls short when we look at God's own activity. It takes hundreds of years for his promised Messiah to come to the world, and Christians are still waiting and waiting for that promised second coming, two thousand years later. God's own patience exasperates and yet more often than not, Christians are willing to give God the benefit of the doubt. We tend to assume that God knows better than we do and that we will find out the plan sooner or later.

What, then, should the potential convert do? A sabbatical is in order—a Sabbath of sorts—to give one time to wait upon God, to see if the urges to leave or stay are confirmed by prayer. Consider those things that might be mistaken for patience and thus give a false sense of patience. Fear can mask as patience when it involves an inability to do something because the consequences seem so great. Apathy and inability to care about others might also mask as patience because one seems to be waiting, but really these denote selfishness and a desire to focus on one's own activities over against caring. To be patient is to wait in hope that the other person may one day come through and experience conversion too.

Praying in Faith

MARTIN LUTHER

From this it follows that the one who prays correctly never doubts that the prayer will be answered, even if the very thing for which one prays is not given. For we are to lay our need before God in prayer but not prescribe to God a measure, manner, time, or place. We must leave that to God, for he may wish to give it to us in another, perhaps better, way than we think best. Frequently we do not know what to pray as St. Paul says in Romans 8, and we know that God's ways are above all that we can ever understand as he says in Ephesians 3. Therefore, we should have no doubt that our prayer is acceptable and heard, and we must leave to God the measure, manner, time, and place, for God will surely do what is right.[1]

1. Luther, "Praying in Faith," 134.

8

Peace

Melissa Musick Nussbaum

Your holiness shall consist of being truly human, not angelic.
God has plenty of angels.

– Kotsker Rebbe

On the evening of Jesus' resurrection, the disciples were in hiding. The cross and the tomb had smashed their dreams. They were terrified that they would be arrested and killed like Jesus. John writes, "Jesus came and stood in their midst and said to them, 'Peace be with you.'"

There was no peace here, and, it would seem, no possibility of peace. Men were cowering, frightened, despairing. The doors were bolted, the blinds pulled. The writer makes this clear, describing "the evening of that first day of the week," as the time "when the doors were locked, for fear . . . " If there was to be peace in that place it had to come from the outside in. The writer says that Jesus came through the locked doors. Jesus brings peace *with* him, and *in* him. It is a gift given to the disciples as a king bestows land—his alone to give—on a chosen courtier.

Jesus says again, "Peace be with you."

No doubt the disciples would have preferred more practical news: that their secret was safe, that they were well concealed from the authorities and that soon they would be able to go back to their nets and fishing boats and tax ledgers. It would be a relief to put this dangerous and fool-hardy adventure behind them.

No sooner has Jesus greeted them a second time, "Peace be with you," than he tells them, "As the Father has sent me, so I send you." We can only imagine their trembling at those words. They are to leave the safety of this room and go out into the very world that holds such menace for them. They are to go among the people they fear. "As the Father has sent me," no longer sounds like a declaration of favor. As the Father sent Jesus now means, they know, arrest and torture and death.

Jesus says, "As the Father has sent me, so I send you." Then he breathes on them, just as God the Father breathed on Adam, bringing him to life. It is an act of creation. Jesus breathes life into them, making them fully human, and sends them out.

The wonder is, they go. They go out into the world. There, so ancient tradition has it, all of them are arrested—like Jesus—and imprisoned—like Jesus. And all, save John the Evangelist, die at the hands of the au-thorities, like Jesus. The fate they fear enough to abandon Jesus and betray him, the fate they seek to avoid in that locked room is finally theirs. The peace with which Jesus sends them forth has nothing to do with safety or security.

The book of Acts tells of Peter's and John's first arraignment before the Sanhedrin after they are seen curing a crippled beggar at the gate of the temple. They are asked, "By what power or by what name have you done this?" (Acts 4:7b).

The same Peter, who crouched low over a courtyard fire and insisted to a servant girl that he did not know the bound and arraigned Jesus of Nazareth, answers them boldly. He denies nothing. He speaks the truth knowing that it may mean his life.

> If we are being examined today about a good deed done to a cripple, namely, by what means he was saved, then all of you and all the people of Israel should know that it was in the name of Jesus Christ the Nazorean whom you crucified, whom God raised from the dead; in his name this man stands before you healed. (Acts 4:9–10)

Here is Peter, publicly identifying himself with a convicted and executed criminal, a man he declares to be God. Not only that, he accuses the men before whom he stands—they with all the power and he with none—of crucifying this Jesus, whom God raised from the dead.

We have no record of Peter's last words before his crucifixion in Rome during the reign of the emperor Nero, but we can imagine that neither his plain speech, nor the peace with which he speaks, failed him. Because there is a peace within Peter unknown to us before Jesus breathes life into him, before the Holy Spirit settles on him like tongues of flame. This peace has nothing to do with safety or security.

That this peace is a gift from God, but a gift without guarantee of safety or security or anything most of us mean by the word "peace," can be understood from Paul's greeting in his letter to the Galatians. He writes, "grace to you and peace from God our Father and the Lord Jesus Christ." He marries grace, or the gifts freely given by God, and peace. Peace comes from God. He certainly could not speak of the peace the Galatians generated. They were torn apart by arguments over doctrine and practice. As Paul writes,

> I am amazed that you are so quickly forsaking the one who called you by the grace of Christ for a different gospel, not that there is another. But there are some who are disturbing you and wish to pervert the gospel of Christ. But if even we or an angel from heaven should preach to you a gospel other than the one we preached to you, let that one be accursed! As we have said before, and now I say again, if anyone preaches to you a gospel other than the one that you received, let that one be accursed! (Gal 1:6–8)

"Forsaken, perverted, accursed," these are not the first words that come to mind when one speaks of peace.

In the Christian tradition, peace is understood as the opposite of chaos and confusion. The locked room in which the disciples are hiding on Easter night is a place of chaos and confusion. They are cut off: from Jesus, from the world and from the life to which they are called. Jesus' presence restores order. He comes in, bringing the world, with him. John writes, "They (the disciples) rejoiced when they saw the Lord" (John 20:20b). Praise replaces fear.

Peace is true order, where not only humans, but all of creation, is in right relationship with God. A tree, as Thomas Merton famously observed, honors God by being a tree. And we honor God—and find peace in right relationship—by being fully human, fully man and fully woman.

In *For the Life of the World*, Alexander Schmemann argues that Jesus of Nazareth "was the perfect expression of life as God intended it."[1] What does this mean? One of the few details we have of Jesus' life is how often he was in prayer: seeking the Father and praising the Father. He lives, moves and has his being in relationship with the Father.

What does this mean for us, who, as individuals, can only be imperfect expressions of life as God intended it? Schmemann writes of us,

> Man is a hungry being. But he is hungry for God. Behind all the hunger of our life is God. All desire is finally a desire for Him . . . the unique position of man in the universe is that he alone is to bless God for the food and the life he receives from Him. He alone is to respond to God's blessing with his blessing . . . "Homo sapiens," "home faber," yes, but first of all, "homo adorans." The first, the basic definition of man is that he is the priest. He stands in the center of the world and unifies it in his act of blessing God, of both receiving the world from God and offering it to God—and by filling the world with his eucharist (thanksgiving), he transforms his life, the one that he receives from the world, into life with God, into communion with Him.[2]

When Peter is denying Christ, he imagines that he is safe. When Peter praises and blesses Christ for the healing of the crippled beggar, he knows is not safe, but he is at peace. When the disciples see Jesus, recognize him as Lord, and rejoice in his presence, they are not safe—the locked door is breached—but they are at peace.

The conflict between our understanding of peace as safety and the church's understanding of peace as right relationship with God, and so with one another, is found throughout Jewish and Christian history. We know Peter was married, because the gospels tell us that Jesus healed his mother-in-law. We do not know if his wife was still living when Peter testified before the Sanhedrin. If she were alive, she may very well have asked him to stay home, stay quiet, stay safe, keep the peace. This confusion of what peace means is common in Scripture. When there is conflict, there is conflict also about what peace means.

In Genesis we hear the story of Joseph and his jealous brothers. Their envy grew, the Scriptures tell us, so that, "When his brothers saw

---

1. Schmemann, *For the Life of the World*, 23.

2. Ibid., 14–15.

that their father loved him best of all his sons, they hated him so much that would not even greet him" (Gen 37:4).

The traditional Hebrew of which the writer speaks is "shalom," or "peace." It is a greeting wishing that all would be well, that is, in right relationship with God, with one another, with the earth. The order of their relationship was so disrupted, so chaotic, that they could no longer even bid one another "peace," let alone live in peace with one another. Their family chaos soon manifests itself in the plot to kill Joseph, a plot that results, finally, not in Joseph's death, but in his being sold into slavery.

Sometimes what peace means for the community and what peace means for the individual come into conflict. In Second Samuel we hear the story of Absalom's revolt against his father and king, David. Joab, one of David's servants, finds Absalom hanging in a tree, his hair caught fast in the branches. Joab stabs him in the heart. He does this for the peace of Israel, for how can the kingdom stand if the king's own son and heir lives as a traitor in their midst?

David is in Jerusalem, between the two gates, waiting for word. The messenger arrives and greets the king. He has good news; right order in Israel has been restored.

> With face to the ground he paid homage to the king and said, "Blessed be the Lord your God, who has delivered up the men who rebelled against my lord the king." (2 Sam 18:28b)

But David has only one question, "Is the youth Absalom safe (shalom)?" It is a father's question, and a father's cry. He wants his son alive; that is the peace for which he longs. Learning of his death, David does not rejoice for the peace (shalom) of Israel. He mourns for his child.

> The king was shaken and went up to the room over the city gate to weep. He said as he wept, "My son Absalom! My son, my son Absalom! If only I had died instead of you, Absalom, my son, my son!" (2 Sam 19:1)

What we desire and what God intends are not one. How we define the right relationship that is peace, is not necessarily either the right relationship or peace. What do Adam and Eve want but to re-order the world God has made, and not in God's image, but in their own? There is no suggestion that they want the resultant chaos we call The Fall. There is no suggestion that they do not want peace, only peace on their terms. In

Adam's and Eve's New Order, they, too, are gods; everyone is a god. The story lasts, always fresh, because it is the ugly secret of every human heart to want to be the god of someone, someplace.

The anger of Joseph's brothers touches us even now, over all these many years, because they want what we all want: to be the favored one, me first, no matter the fate of others.

David's cries pierce us even now, over all these many years, because he wants what all parents want: my child first, my child well, my child kept from harm, no matter the fate of other children.

Peace is relational. It is a state of being in harmony with the Other, God, and with others, our brothers and sisters. A person can have self-control alone or patience alone. She may be kind to those who are unkind. He may be faithful to those who are unfaithful. But peace is communal. Joseph may greet his brothers with, "Shalom," but, if they cannot reply in kind, the peace of the household is broken.

No sooner does the writer of Acts recount Peter's testimony before the Sanhedrin than he returns us to the life of the Jerusalem church, Peter's church. He writes,

> The community of believers was of one heart and mind, and no one claimed that any of his possessions was his own, but they had everything in common. (Acts 4:32)

Peter is in right relationship with God and with his brothers and sisters. They are "of one heart and mind." There is peace.

The fact of leaving one church or one denomination for another means that the peace, the right order, of the household has been broken. No doubt that peace is broken long before the actual leave-taking, beginning with the first stirrings of alienation. Christians live with this scandal—*in* this scandal—every day. Jesus prays that we "may be one as the Father and I are one" (John 17:22b), and yet we are scattered, atomized, divided into more and deeper separations. Our communions are closed to one another, the very table of God denied to all the children of God. We do not begin our communal life of Christian faith in communal peace. How can we expect to find peace in yet another separation?

It is critical in this situation of chaos and confusion that we, like Jesus, persist in prayer: seeking God and praising God. As we move farther and farther from one another, the temptation is to leave the practices that once united us—and that can unite us again—behind. We must look to Jesus. As he hangs on the cross and calls out to God, asking why he has been forsaken, Jesus still prays. It is to the Father alone he calls. He calls out in pain. He calls out from the darkness. He calls out in abandonment. But the very act of calling out to God is an act of relationship, an act of abiding. Jesus does not suffer alone, and neither must we.

It may be that, like Joseph and his brothers, we will have to wait a very long time for peace. We may have to endure famine and exile before we can find our way to God's right order for his household.

Still, in the midst of the brokenness, we can strive to remain, simply, who we are, "homo adorans." Man the thinker, man the maker, but first, man the one who adores God. We can acknowledge that there is a God, and we are not God. We can acknowledge that all life is a gift from God and that our primary responsibility—even when we, like the disciples are in the chaos of fear and anger and separation—is to see the Lord come into our locked rooms and to rejoice. We can praise God, confessing, even as we do, our divisions and hostilities.

Schmemann writes, "It is not 'grace' that comes down; it is the Church that enters into 'grace.'"[3] In praising God, even behind the locked doors of a broken communion, we enter into grace. We enter that grace together, all of us who praise, even if on every other level of doctrine and practice, we are at odds.

When I was pregnant with my fourth child, I joined a women's Bible study. I joined the Bible study for two reasons: it was close to my house and they had a good childcare program. The church was not my own, and there were many points on which I stood in profound disagreement with their teachings.

The morning of our first gathering, the leader addressed us. She acknowledged the different varieties of Christians who had assembled. And she told us, "If we can confess Christ as Lord, we can, at the very least, begin to walk and pray together." It was not the peace for which we must, and do, pray, for which we must, and do, work. It was not the whole of creation in harmony. But it was we women, together, praising God. It was, it is, the beginning of peace.

---

3. Schmemann, *For the Life of the World*, 31.

A Simple Regimen of Private Prayer
GEORGE BUTTRICK

Then may follow a prayer of *intercession*, without which the most earnest prayer might sink into selfishness. *The Lord's Prayer* in almost every phrase keeps us mindful of our neighbors: *"Our* Father" . . . *"our* daily bread" . . . *"our* trespasses."

Private intercession should be specific. "We humbly beseech Thee for all sorts and conditions of people," is an appropriate phrase in a collect—which, as the very word indicates, draws all worshipers into one act of devotion, and provides a form into which each worshiper may pour his secret prayer—but it is out of place in individual petition.

Genuine love sees faces, not a mass: the good shepherd the good shepherd "calleth his own sheep by name." Intercession is more than specific: it is pondered: it requires us to bear on our heart the burden of those for whom we pray.[1]

1. Buttrick, "A Simple Regimen of Prayer," 102.

9

Joy

JANA MARGUERITE BENNETT

*We were created to delight, as God does,
in the resident goodness of creation.*

– Robert Farrar Capon

At least once a year, I have students in one of my theology classes read the account of the martyrdom of Perpetua and Felicity.[1] These two young women, not coincidentally about the students' own ages, were second-century people arrested for being Christians, thrown into prison, and eventually sentenced to death. The account is unique in that part of it is Perpetua's own story and her own recounting of dreams she had before she was tried and executed. She and Felicity both believed that despite all the hardships they would inevitably experience in the stadium (wild animals attacking them to the death), they had the certainty of an eternal and happy life.

> I beheld a ladder of bronze, marvelously great, reaching up to heaven; and it was narrow, so that not more than one might go up at one time. And in the sides of the ladder were planted all manner of things of iron. There were swords there, spears, hooks, and

1. Perpetua, *The Passion of Perpetua and Felicity*. W. H. Shewring's 1931 translation of this text can be found online at Paul Halsall's Medieval Sourcebook website: http://www.fordham.edu/halsall/source/perpetua.html.

> knives; so that if any that went up took not good heed or looked not upward, he would be torn and his flesh cling to the iron. And there was right at the ladder's foot a serpent lying, marvelously great, which lay in wait for those that would go up, and frightened them that they might not go up . . . And I said: it shall not hurt me, in the name of Jesus Christ. And from beneath the ladder, as though it feared me, it softly put forth its head; and as though I trod on the first step I trod on its head. And I went up, and I saw a very great space of garden, and in the midst a man sitting, white-headed, in shepherd's clothing, tall milking his sheep; and standing around in white were many thousands. And he raised his head and beheld me and said to me: Welcome, child.[2]

But the certainty of eternal life was more than just a hoped-for longing for the future; it radically affected the ways the two women behaved at their execution. Death by wild animal took quite a bit of time; in the middle of the execution, when the animals had been called off for the moment, Perpetua was startled and astonished to discover that animals had already begun attacking her, for she herself was already experiencing a certain kind of joy—the delights of being with people in heaven.

> As now awakening from sleep (so much was she in the Spirit and in ecstasy) began first to look about her; and then (which amazed all there), When, forsooth, she asked, are we to be thrown to the cow? And when she heard that this had been done already, she would not believe till she perceived some marks of mauling on her body and on her dress. Thereupon she called her brother to her, and that catechumen, and spoke to them, saying: Stand fast in the faith, and love you all one another; and be not offended because of our passion.[3]

My students are always struck by how much joy these martyrs appeared to experience. "I wouldn't be too joyful myself if I were facing a wild animal . . ."

The early martyrs' joy is one that puzzles, for it conflicts with what modern people typically understand as joy. Being tortured to death, and in pain, is not something that we would tend to embrace joyfully, to say the least. In fact, many elements in American and Northern European culture are devoted to removing pain and extending life: drugs abound,

2. Ibid.
3. Ibid.

not simply for serious cancer cases, but also for the minor headache that needs precisely the right formula to erase headache pain. The notion of self-medicating on recreational drugs like alcohol can also serve the purpose of removing pain from our immediate experience.

The joy Perpetua and Felicity have is also perplexing because it does not quite count as joy by modern accounts. If we think of joy at all, we tend to think of a euphoric state of physical and mental well-being. In other words, the common use of "joy" suggests that it is a sort of souped-up version of the word "happy." We have rather more romanticized versions of joy. Church banners are especially notorious for proclaiming this kind of joy: I once had a rainbow and a large fabric heart and the words "Joy, Joy, Joy!" emblazoned on it in gold lettering, more reminiscent of an eight-year-old girl's fantasy land than a theological statement. Joy is often equated with euphoria: the ultimate in happiness, gladness, even glee, and the assumption often seems to be that if a church member isn't smiling a hundred-watt smile in worship, something must be amiss. Sometimes people, especially those who are unhappy with their Christian communities, are advised to "grin and bear it," or they think they *ought* to be happy, any case, and suffer in silence with the church while putting a plasticized, public smile on things.

In conjunction with this overly ebullient view of joy comes the question: do we really want joy? Joy in the martyrs' sense is almost too terrible to bear for many, and the plasticized view of joy is too hard to bear as well. How can we express joy even in the face of wrongs done and evil perpetuated? Perhaps what we modern people really want is not true joy but satisfaction—we want to be able to satisfy our hunger, our thirst, and desire for a place to sleep at night. Our desire for satisfaction goes beyond simple material wants, however: we want the satisfaction of knowing justice is done and that punishment, at the least, has been exacted for any wrongs committed. We want the satisfaction of having answers to unanswerable questions about why evil and dissension exists in the world. If something bad or problematic has happened, we want the satisfaction of having someone or something to blame for the medical disaster or the legal snafu or the political crisis or the feud with the next door neighbor.

If satisfaction is indeed what we modern people seek over joy, then the central questions of this book, about staying in or leaving a Christian communion, become even more troublesome. It is easy to put blame on the community one wants to leave; it is easy to seek being "satisfied" in a congregation by finding just the one that meets "my" needs and "my" desires. The person who is reading this book likely wants to avoid those pitfalls and yet the difficult questions must be faced, especially when confronting staying or leaving. How can we think of joy in the face of lack of communion in the Christian community? Can leaving one Christian community for another ever truly cause joy? For it seems that to rejoice in something that is sorrowful—that has torn apart families for centuries—must be wrong.

At the heart of questions about leaving are questions about ecumenism and its own problems. After all, people would not need even to face the question of leaving one communion for another if ecumenism worked in the way we think it ought to work. As William Rusch has suggested, the assumed goal of ecumenism is unity, expressed as *koinonia* and *communio* in World Council of Churches documents.[4] When people leave one communion for another, particularly for those communions that do not grant full Eucharistic communion, it puts all Christians face-to-face once again with the knowledge that most Christians do not, in fact, hold all things in common. For some, the insinuation may even be, "He just thought *that* church was better . . ." Accusations can then abound about whether someone is church shopping, church hopping, and the like. One evangelical pastor muses on the fact that many people leave one church for another and writes in a blog,

> In my study so far I have not found any Scriptural support at all for viewing the local church with the mindset of a consumer, where I join because of what the church offers me and I stay so long as "my needs" are being met to my satisfaction. I haven't seen any examples in the Scripture of someone moving to another church because they had better worship, a bigger children's ministry, more choices for Sunday School, a more eloquent preacher, or even because "I feel led by the Holy Spirit."[5]

One lament of those working in ecumenical circles through the decades has been the sense that Christians can only put their best face forward when they are in union. Christians who think of leaving communion for another cannot possibly be demonstrating unity, but disunity, so "grinning" and "bearing" whatever problems one has with a communion

---

4. Rusch, "A Survey of Ecumenical Reflection about Unity," 9.
5. Conant, "Thought for the Week July 13 2008."

is often seen as the best and most responsible manifestation of Christian action.[6] Might this, too, be some version of that euphoric, plasticized joy? And, against the charge of church shopping, might there be occasions when someone really is called by God to another communion so that the joy experienced is confirmation of that call?

Church banners notwithstanding, the Christian use of joy is something quite different than a maxed-out emotion or the mere appearance of happiness. The story of the martyrs gives us one hint of that: their joy comes not from some bizarre sadistic ideal but from a certain knowledge that this life is God's. It seems, in fact, that church shopping is an example of the fruits of a false joy that causes dissension, over against a real joy that might even be beneficial and fruitful for ecumenical dialogue.

Church leaders have long despaired over the Western phenomenon of what is commonly called "church shopping." British author Nigel Scotland notes that a culture of consumerism "has created a generation of church shoppers who move from one fellowship to another in the same way that grocery shoppers change from Tesco's to Safeways to Sainsbury's to Waitrose to Gateway and back."[7] With a consumer mentality, people are encouraged to emphasize their own wants and needs and that "Jesus will make them happy and fulfilled."[8] Individual satisfaction looms large, and it is proper to ask whether and how that satisfaction relates to Paul's sense of joy.

Paul's letter to the Galatians underscores the activity of God in the fruit of the Spirit by putting the fruits of the Spirit directly in contrast with what he calls "works of the flesh": "immorality, impurity, licentiousness,

6. Though he has a slightly different view of ecumenical dialogue and breaking fellowship with a Christian communion, Ephraim Radner is one theologian that I think holds this kind of view. For him, the best witness any Christian can give in our post-Christian, decidedly disunified world is to accede to the fact that Christ's Body, the church, is a broken body, and we who live in broken communion necessarily suffer in this Body. Radner is not proposing the kind of false happiness I discuss above, but his thinking does still lend itself to a particular brand of "grin and bear it." I am sympathetic with much that Radner suggests, but I worry that his proposals omit the possibility that God might, in fact, be calling a person or congregation out of one communion and into another. Our contention in this book is that leaving one Christian communion for another is a horrible sort of discernment, but sometimes a more obedient move. See Radner's book *The End of the Church*, or his essays in the recent discussion of the Anglican Church's current crisis in Radner and Turner, *The Fate of Communion*.

7. Scotland, "Shopping for a Church," 144.

8. Ibid., 145.

idolatry, sorcery, hatreds, rivalry, jealousy, outbursts of fury, acts of self-ishness, dissensions, factions, occasions of envy, drinking bouts, orgies, and the like" (Gal 5:19). Works seem more human-driven, but fruits are Spirit-driven. Thus, the kind of "joy" that is mostly centered on human emotion or human-based action seems not to be the kind of joy that Paul envisions. But of course, one of the questions that must be raised is how to avoid the plasticized, romantic and euphoric ideas of joy and allow the Spirit's joy to be present instead.

If the fruit of discernment is joy, and if that fruit cannot be the initial euphoric feelings but instead is manifested in a deeper attachment to a community, then the question is raised: how can a person ever leave? Isn't leaving, in a sense, always about seeking something better, which seems dangerously close to those euphoric feelings?

There is some debate over whether "conversion" is the most appropriate word to use when we speak of Christians moving from one church to another. Ultimately, one cannot give a fully intellectual reason (or at least not an intellectually satisfying reason). The reason is that conversion, a word that means "turning toward," involves turning toward a different set of practices, beliefs, and ways of living. Those new ways of living entail different ways of thinking—ways of thinking that cannot necessarily be reconciled intelligibly to those who share the former way of life. Conversion will not make sense at some point, for either the one converting or the one staying.

An article from *The Christian Century* makes this clear. Jason Byassee, one of the magazine's editors, wrote an article commenting on the extraordinary fact that six prominent theologians had recently left various Protestant denominations for the Roman Catholic Church. Three were Lutherans, two were Anglicans, and one was a Mennonite. Byassee struggles throughout the article with accounting for how it is that these six would leave their respective churches. Rusty Reno, a former Anglican, stands out for him because Reno wrote an entire book called *In the Ruins of the Church*, in which he argues that the faithful thing to do is to stay in one's church, despite all its shortcomings—to maintain a resolute commitment to abide with whatever original community one had. To do otherwise would be to cave in to personal preferences. So, when Reno became a Roman Catholic, it was a momentous event: the one arguing that people should remain in their churches was the one doing the leaving. Byassee comments, "It's unclear how Reno made this move without indulging the modernist temptations—listening to one's feelings, being impatient with institutions, believing things are better elsewhere—that he describes so well in *In the Ruins*."[9]

It is understandable that Byassee and other people would be perplexed by moves from one church to another. What is it, after all, that appears so great about the one over the other? Friends and family members, and the potential convert himself, will wrestle with that question. But in conversion, as with much in life, there must be room for the possibility that God is moving a person toward a new life. In fact, by some accounts, that is precisely who God is: the one who "is making all things new" (Rev 21:5).

Still, the question Byassee and others raise is valid. Part of the answer, I think, is to recognize what the idealized versions of joy might look like and to discern as far as possible the extent to which an impulse to stay or leave is driven by an idealized joy. C. S. Lewis's *Screwtape Letters* is a series of letters between Uncle Screwtape, a senior demon in Hell, and his junior colleague, Wormwood. The two demons are monitoring a human (their "patient") who has become newly Christian and is reveling in the joy of that conversion. The demons are, understandably, concerned that their human subject has decided to become Christian and they ponder ways to make his conversion less significant so that they can win him to their side. Screwtape compares the ideal version of Christianity to the reality, and suggests that Wormwood use that discrepancy. Screwtape writes,

> Make his mind flit to and fro between an expression like 'the body of Christ' and the actual faces in the next pew. . . . Provided that any of those neighbours sing out of tune, or have boots that squeak, or double chins, or odd clothes, the patient will quite easily believe that their religion must therefore be somehow ridiculous. At his present stage, you see, he has an idea of 'Christian' in his mind which he supposes to be spiritual but which, in fact, is largely pictorial.[10]

Similarly to the emotions that Wormwood's patient experiences, joy often comes across as a necessary part of an ideal experience. Wormwood's "uncle demon" is very smart: he knows that, for the most part, such idealism cannot last when confronted with the reality of dishes in the sink, or

9. Byassee, "Going Catholic," 18.
10. Lewis, *Screwtape Letters*, 6.

bills that are past due or the old car that continually needs repair. Adult faith does not remain in that land of rainbows, and Screwtape knows that a focus on the mundane is indeed a fast way to make people second-guess their decisions, even life-changing decisions like becoming Christian.

A friend of mine, Andrew, was raised in the Reformed tradition but considered becoming Eastern Orthodox for a time. He was concerned about his Reformed congregation for many reasons: the contemporary praise music they sang week after week seemed a bit too fluffy, there wasn't enough reverence on the part of the parishioners, and the prayers, written by the pastor, seemed to be more about his personal whims about what the congregation ought to know than about prayer to God. From Andrew's perspective, Orthodoxy answered some of these faults. Here was a church where all of the prayers seemed deeply significant; they probed the mystery of God in ways that the praise music never had. The very length of the service (two hours or more), the use of incense, the bowing before the cross and icons, and the continual singing and chanting suggested to him a more reverent attitude than he had known. Moreover, the entire service was centuries-old, and had been prayed over and over again in churches since at least the fifth century; here was no passing whim.

Andrew's infatuation stage with Orthodoxy lasted a few years. He bought books by prominent Greek and Russian Orthodox theologians; he bought the service book of the Divine Liturgy in Greek so that he could follow along at the Greek-speaking church; he went to as many Orthodox services as he could manage. He began to attend introductory classes for people considering Orthodoxy, and he made appointments with several priests to speak with them about becoming Orthodox. Just as a lover seeks to know as much about his beloved as possible, Andrew sought after the Orthodox Church and doing so gave him a kind of joy, precisely because he was rejoicing in something he cared about and loved and he was expressing that care and love.

We should pause here a moment, because I am sure that readers will readily see where the point will end: euphoric feelings are not substantial enough to sustain a relationship, nor do they amount to "true joy." But to jump too readily ahead to that point is to miss that the infatuation and initial feelings are important to the discernment for leaving and staying, particularly if a person has been motivated to consider leaving out of love for another communion and another way of worshipping. For most people, I suspect that conversion or considering becoming some "other kind" of Christian requires that kind of euphoria initially. This is a time for young romance, when infatuation leads you to want to know and embrace everything about the other church. The attraction is what sparks the interest in the first place, just as with a new dating relationship or teenage crush. Everything "there" in that other church seems fabulous; everything "here" seems problematic and there is a certain kind of "joy" in that euphoria, that initial seeking out answers to problems.

There usually comes a point in love relationships where there is a test of that kind of joy. The cracks show through; the person you thought you married turned out to be not quite the "Claire Huxtable" model mother and wife you were hoping for. After a while, Andrew started noticing the three or four families standing in the back of the church who would talk to each other throughout the entire service, looking bored, and generally treating the Eucharist without the reverence and mystery that he believed needed to be attached to it. And he noticed that as he became more and more familiar with the chants, the worship service became less enticing and it lost its newness. In other words, he found himself confronted with the question of how to live with the congregation for the long term— the same question that he had back when he was attending a Reformed church, as he later pointed out to me. The initial joyful euphoria, the joy on the surface, was replaced with the humdrum of life in a congregation.

At the end of it all, Andrew found himself unable to discern for or against either communion. This, I think, was the move of a very mature individual. He recognized that the "choice" he had to make was not between the Reformed congregation and the Orthodox community. Rather, he had the important task of figuring out the difference between making a choice based on satisfaction (our culture's pseudo-sense of joy), and seeing whether God might actually be calling him to a different communion. Instead of allowing the question to be polarized further, he began attending the Episcopalian Church close to where he lives, and is still discerning whether to make a more determinative move to belong to that congregation.

One way to test the extent of "satisfaction" as motivation for leaving one communion for another is to place yourself in a position that might be less than satisfactory. A colleague of mine says of Christian conversions, "Before you join, be sure you attend a year's worth of bad worship in that church." A superficial or even false joy objectifies both communions, but neither can likely withstand the strictures of that objectification. This is one way of deliberately juxtaposing some of the worst of the new tradition with the euphoric feelings in hopes of striking a balance and avoiding overly romantic notions of a church.

In contrast to this ideal but false joy, we might think of the parables of the lost and found as examples of the kind of joy a Christian has: the parables of the lost sheep and the lost coin involve a seeker who is focused on a singular purpose—that of finding the object that was lost—and is overjoyed when it is found. In both these stories, joy comes partly because of the work involved in the search. I imagine the woman looking for the lost coin, for example, overturning boxes, checking in places again and again, going over every inch of every surface with a magnifying glass. And the shepherd looking for the lost sheep leaves all the other sheep behind just to find the one that is lost. The other sheep might also have run away or become victim to the wolves, but the shepherd does not give a thought to them, and rejoices greatly when the one sheep he has sought is found. It is the intensity of the searches that strikes me here—the grief that comes with losing something precious is matched by a deep desire to have that object restored. Christians considering joining a different communion are also searchers who display similar intensity. One telling point here, however, is that these parables speak of people seeking after the same object that they have lost. One of the difficulties with a "search" for another Christian community is that it often ends in a search for a different object to replace the one that is "lost."

Also striking is that neither the woman nor the shepherd can have any assurance, while searching, that they will find the object, but they do not give up. There is an aspect of the search that is out of their control—though they do everything they can do retrieve the lost objects, still the moment of joy will not come solely by the act of searching. It comes in part because of grace. That the coin or the sheep are found is a gift, not an assurance. So too, one is *gifted* by finding a Christian community, and there is a significant part of the search that should have little to do with the "work" of the seeker.

Joy is not really an individual fruit, just as none of the other fruits of the Spirit can be observed individualistically. When we read about joy in the Scriptures, they remind us again and again of the communal nature of joy.

Paul writes about joy in his letter to the Romans, and relates it to love. "Do not by your eating destroy your brother for whom Christ died.

Do not allow what you consider good to be spoken of as evil. For the kingdom of God is not a matter of eating and drinking, but of righteousness, peace and joy in the Holy Spirit . . ." (Rom 14:15–17). Joy, suggests Paul, is not a matter of getting caught up in the correctness of one's arguments, but is instead given by the Holy Spirit. So again, we come back to the point that joy is more a joy in God and God's actions in one's life, rather than a sensation felt.

Uncle Screwtape takes a bet on the fact that Wormwood's "patient" will not think to probe very deeply beyond surface affection and beyond his own internal pathos. The magnificence of the idea of "Body of Christ" will pale, he hopes, besides the annoyance of squeaky boots and bad hymnody. Unfortunately for Screwtape and Wormwood, the "patient" sees through the superficiality of his initial feelings and becomes an even more committed Christian. The patient has realized that the superficiality of his feelings have revolved largely around himself, but the joy of being Christian comes more in having that fruit despite, or even because of, other peoples' foibles (and one's own).

Getting beyond the superficiality requires seeing that the people in the pew are, like the "patient," strangely, incomprehensibly, and even humorously, the ones God has chosen to be witnesses of Christ's presence in the world. He has come to realize that he is not entitled to be part of some perfect, idealized "Body of Christ" but has instead been called to be part of the Body as God has given it. We think of God as awesome, all-good, all-powerful, and all-knowing, and so it is a bit of a mind-bender to figure out why God should choose imperfect humans to be witnesses. The Scriptures are full of such examples, however: Moses, the murderer, is the one God chooses to lead the people from slavery in Egypt. Jeremiah, the complainer, is the one God chooses to prophecy to the Israelites. David, the adulterer, is God's chosen king for the Chosen People. Saul, the violent persecutor, becomes Paul, the missionary witness for Christ and author of half the New Testament. Part of the realization Screwtape's patient (and any convert) has to make is that imperfection, and even sin, does not equal inability to be part of God's life. If we hold on too tightly to the idea that God's community must look and act a certain way, we shall never see the true oddity and mystery of that very community.

When Wormwood's patient becomes a more "committed Christian" it is because he has recognized his superficial feelings, but has also come to love the people in his community because they are also God's witnesses.

The joy that comes as a fruit of the Spirit comes when one can no longer vilify one congregation and magnify another by way of contrasting the two. Rather the Spirit's joy comes in seeing the people in both communities as human and as in relationship with God as best as they know how.

I Will Lie Down This Night

Melissa Musick Nussbaum

It is tempting to think of the examination of conscience at the end of the day as a kind of score sheet—Visitors 5, Home 0—to be entered into the heavenly ledger, with the end of time as the final grand and glorious reconciling of the human tally. And, as with all scores, it is tempting to settle some and contest others. "Yes, I did smack the baby's bottom, but it was only after . . ." and the argument commences. We uncover, in a striptease of the conscience, strategically, and then scramble to gather up and restore our covering. It is too fearsome to admit nakedness.

But nakedness is what we are, in truth, invited into in the examination of conscience. To learn in nakedness is to lie in nakedness, as one lies still under the soft, exploring touch of the beloved, and to reveal oneself—marked, flawed, scarred, misshapen—and to begin to understand that the beloved alters not, withdraws never, when it alteration finds.

It is the image Jesus gives us of the prodigal son: ill-clad, ill-fed and having squandered all his father's gifts, embraced in his father's arms, standing close under his father's gaze. The son cannot conceal the toll of the road—its odor, its dusting of grit and streaky sheen of sweat—nor can he produce what he does not have, the lost fortune. With neither the means nor the strength for concealment, the son had to choose: To come at all was to come stripped and naked. Yet the Father does not withdraw or turn away. He sees, and loves.[1]

---

1. Nussbaum, *I Will Lie Down This Night*, 53–55.

10

Love

MELISSA MUSICK NUSSBAUM

It was said of Abba John the Persian that when some evildoers came to him, he took a basin and wanted to wash their feet. But they were filled with confusion and began to do penance.

– *Sayings of the Desert Fathers*

According to ancient tradition, the apostle John survived his imprisonment on Patmos and went on to serve as the Bishop of Ephesus. There, so the story goes, his flock had only one complaint. They were tired of hearing the same sermon over and over. Every Sunday, John would rise and preach, "Little children, let us love one another."

Some members of the church went to John. "Bishop," they implored, "Could we please have a new sermon?"

"Of course," he replied, "Of course I will preach a new sermon. Just as soon as we learn this one."

Two thousand years is a long learning curve. A learning curve refers to a relationship between the length of learning time and evidence that the lesson has, in fact, been learned. If Bishop John were alive today, he would still be preaching the same sermon.

We may agree on what love means, but not on what love does. And though Christians have practically trademarked the word love, the question of what it does—for that is, finally, the only question—divides us.

When Moses sees a bush on Mount Horeb that is on fire, but not consumed by the fire, he hears God calling to him. God says,

> I have witnessed the affliction of my people in Egypt and have heard their cry of complaint against their slave drivers, so I know well what they are suffering. Therefore I have come down to rescue them from the hands of the Egyptians and lead them out of that land into a good and spacious land, a land flowing with milk and honey. (Exod 3:7–8a)

Witnessed, heard, come down to rescue—God is revealed to Moses as One who acts in history, as One who acts to save. God does not wish us well; God comes into our midst and sets us free.

But count on this: In most church disputes, with those who stay and those who leave, all involved will use the word "loving" to describe his actions, to describe her attitude. Those with whom they are in conflict or disagreement will be described as "unloving."

That is why I do not want to discuss the more exalted uses of the word "love," but to ask, rather, what does it look like to love one another, and to love one another, as John of Ephesus has it, without conditions of either affection or agreement? There is no admonition to love those who love us, or to love those we admire. In Matthew's gospel, Jesus cautions, "You have heard that it was said, You shall love your neighbor and hate your enemy. But I say to you, love your enemies and pray for those who persecute you . . ." (5:43–44)

John's sermon, though less inclusive than Christ's, is addressed to the "little children," that is, the followers, *all* the followers, of Christ. "Little children, let us love one another." It reads as a one-sentence rule.

In vowed religious life, a rule refers to a set of regulations regarding the life of the community. It sets out how guests are to be welcomed—or asked to leave—how the sick are to be treated, how food is to be shared. The rule spells out how Christians show their love for one another, not on thoughts or feelings, but in clean underwear and welcome tables and weeded gardens.

A rule is the foundation and framework upon which a Christian life is constructed. Among the two best-known rules for religious life are the Rule of St. Augustine, written about the year 400, and the Rule of St. Benedict, written between 530 and 560. Written and put into practice long before the schism separating Protestants and Catholics, the rules remain a resource for Christians of many denominations and traditions.

When those who follow either the Rule of Augustine or the Rule of Benedict speak of their lives, they speak of "keeping" the rule. Keep is an old word, as in "Remember, keep holy the Sabbath." We may rest on Sunday or turn off the television or devote the day to scripture reading and study, but we seldom use the words "keep holy the Sabbath" anymore, unless we are quoting from the Ten Commandments. We speak of going to services, or Mass or going to church. My grandparents and parents kept company. My husband and I did not keep company. We dated. Our children date, but they are more likely to speak of hanging out.

It's interesting to think of all that we do still keep. We keep books, entering withdrawals and deposits. We keep records, of a child's vaccinations, of the last time the furnace was checked, of the oil change schedule. We keep diaries and day planners, accounts of appointments and dinner engagements and birthdays and anniversaries. Musicians keep time, tapping out the quarter notes and dotted eighths that establish rhythm. We try to keep up appearances, showering and shaving and dressing in clean clothes, the daily personal care so like the daily house care. Mostly, we keep track—of our children's soccer games, our caloric intake, and our vacation days.

Look back at the list; we keep routines, the routines of tasks and days that will come round again and again, as long as we live. We clean the refrigerator, knowing it will have to be cleaned again. We take the baby to the pediatrician for the DPT shot, knowing we will be back for the booster. We mark Thanksgiving and are surprised when it comes—so soon—once more.

And, in religious life, the members still speak of keeping a rule. Perhaps those in religious life continue to speak of keeping the rule because the rule is so practical, so domestic and so daily. Not a word about world domination, but a strong word about what used to be called "custody of the eyes." For us, custody of the eyes covers everything from how we lust after another's wife to how we lust after a neighbor's plasma television.

There's not a word about sweeping changes in the health care system, but a lot about how sick people, and the ones who care for them, are called to behave. And there is little about the emotion, or feeling, of love, but much about the daily, hourly keeping that permits and nourishes love. Notice that a rule is all about what we do, and not about what we think.

Just as dusting is an act, and not a thought, so keeping the rule is an action, or a series of actions.

Parents understand how the work of love is prior to any thought or talk of love. A mother may speak without ceasing of the great love she feels for her child, but if she is not feeding him or holding him when he cries or changing his diapers or protecting him from the cold, we can be sure that his perception of the relationship will be marked, not by the mother's caring, but by her killing carelessness. It is this wisdom that informs the ancient Christian rules. It is a wisdom that understands Christian life does not exist in different forms, one for church and one for home. The lessons of the household are lessons for the church. The lessons of the church are lessons for the household.

People who have never read or followed a rule might expect it to be, well, more spiritual, something on the order of "Love, love is all you need." The trouble with all that love talk, of course, is that we are members of families and communities and parishes and congregations. We have neighbors and friends, and we know very well the pain caused by people who love us, and believe that's all we need. Most of us have, at one time or another, been, as the saying goes, "loved to death." We have all heard of the man, on trial for the murder of his girlfriend, who sobs that he simply "loved her too much," and it was love leading him to the gun or the knife. The *feeling* of love, intense when it advances and intense when it retreats, can turn a life-giving river into a fatal flood. The lessons of daily life are lessons for the church.

Before Augustine ever uses the word "love," he uses the word "harmony." Just as Paul, in his letter to the Galatians, uses the word "peace," before he ever uses the word "love." Because, in fact, a rule, like love itself—just ask any long-married couple—is mostly about housekeeping duties, the sorts of things necessary to harmony in a community: meals and laundry and finances and illness and doing what you're asked without grumbling. (Augustine talks about grumbling much more than he talks about love.) The stuff of the rule is mostly familiar to the housekeeper.

In eight chapters of his rule, St. Augustine only uses the word "love" five times, and not once in his statement of "the first purpose." "The first purpose for which you have come together is to live in unity in the house and be of one mind and heart on the way to God." He says nothing about loving the brothers and sisters who are to come together in unity. He says nothing about loving the brothers and sisters who are to be of one mind and heart on the way to God. And that's because Augustine is no fool. He knows that love, like an orderly house, like matched socks, is an end. But the way to the orderly house, and the way to love, lies in small acts, little tasks, done daily.

Rule keepers are housekeepers. And a rule is a little mirror, in which we can catch our reflections as we keep house. It's not for admiration; there's little to admire in proper sweeping technique. The mirror is there to help us learn. The rule functions like a parent or a coach or a piano teacher, saying, "Watch me and then you do it." Rule keepers are house-keepers, and the house is the community.

Rules are predicated on the idea that people will remain in one place, with the same people, until death. Our book is predicated on the idea that some people will leave one Christian community for another. What does a rule for religious life have to say about love to Christians who are leaving a church, or to the Christians who are left? How can it address those who can no longer "be of one mind and heart on the way to God"? We begin to find the answer, I think, not in searching to retrieve an agreement that no longer exists, but in behavior. We need to practice right behavior even when the feelings are all wrong.

The Rule of St. Augustine never assumes goodwill or good feelings among the brothers. The whole of chapter 6 is devoted to "Asking Pardon and Forgiving Offense." The writer assumes offenses will be committed and human love will fail. He begins the chapter with a warning:

> You should either avoid quarrels altogether or else put an end to them as quickly as possible; otherwise, anger may grow into hatred, making a plank out of a splinter, and turn the soul into a murderer. For so you read: *Everyone who hates his brother is a murderer.* (1 John 3:15)

Notice that Augustine says nothing about civilized disagreements, the good-natured debate. He writes about quarrels and contention, anger and hostility. No one has to be in love with laundry—and one can petition for another job—but laundry must be done, for the good of the community. It's the middle-of-the-night-throw-up rule, well known to all parents: I don't have to be happy about waking to a screaming child and a filthy crib, all demanding my immediate and sympathetic attention, but I do have to get up and do the work. Alcoholics Anonymous might have written their famous phrase for members of families and churches:

"Fake it 'til you make it." Even if you hate, act like a person who loves. St. Augustine writes,

> Whoever has injured another by open insult, or by abusive or even incriminating language, must remember to repair the injury as quickly as possible by an apology, and he who suffered the injury must also forgive, without further wrangling. [For, he continues] a brother who is never willing to ask pardon, or does not do so from his heart, has no reason to be in the monastery, even if he is not expelled.

Forgiving and asking forgiveness, Augustine seems to say, is part of the housework, the housekeeping, of Christian life. Everyone has to take part, the offender and the offended. No one is exempt. Like taking out the trash or cleaning the toilet, it is necessary, messy and often unpleasant work. The one who isn't willing to lend a hand, whether to yard work or forgiveness work, doesn't belong in the church to begin with, even if he has caused no problems. Why? Because this work, this forgiving and being forgiven is what we do. It's who we are. It is the work of love, the work *to* love, and it is the only way we know. It is the only way we are given.

There was an ugly church dispute. I was involved, as was a neighbor of mine. I was walking through the park when I spotted her. I wanted to turn and walk the other way, but it was too late. She had seen me, just as I had seen her. When we drew abreast of one another, she greeted me and introduced me to her dog. She told me a funny story about the animal, and after enough time had passed to call the encounter polite, she and I said our good-byes and walked on. There was no reconciliation, but there was courtesy and courage—and all on her part—and what Paul would call "gentleness." She saw me and recognized me and acted in a way I know to have required great charity and self-control on her part. Was it love? It was certainly not affection, but it was the work, however modest, that alone makes love possible. I know her behavior softened my heart towards her, and made me less willing to believe the hateful things my circle in the dispute were willing to share, and I to repeat.

Our book never assumes a person leaving the Christian church altogether. So we are still, in whatever Christian tradition, the "little children" of Christ, and so bound by the mutual labor that is love. A church nearby is in the middle of a bitter split, involving lawsuits and police calls. A group of men who have been together for years in a Bible study, elected to remain together. They are divided, some of them worshipping in the church building, others gathering in a rented space. Their meetings have a tension that is new and uncomfortable for them all. There are topics they cannot discuss, questions they cannot ask. Yet, when the time came for the annual fall clean up of the original church property, they all agreed to meet in a place many had left with bitter words. Together, they would rake and mulch and do the work necessary to keep the grounds through the long winter.

This story continues. I do not know how it will end. The divisions are real and deep. These men may never again share the affection they once knew. But, if they refused to do the work of love, they would foreclose even the possibility of reconciliation. By doing the work of love, as awkward and onerous as it may be, they have done what may keep the scattered seeds of communion through their long winter.

Conclusion: There Is Life after Conversion

Jana Marguerite Bennett

A few years ago, my husband Joel was received into full communion with the Roman Catholic Church. It was a difficult move for both of us. I had joined the Catholic Church just two years before and remembered well how that placed a wedge between me and my family. Joel's family was, likewise, not altogether thrilled at the prospect of having a Catholic son.

It was difficult for me too, because I did not want for him to become Catholic if his reason was because I was Catholic. I am sure there are members of both his and my families that wonder if that was, in fact, his reason. But at the time I thought I wanted him to make a "free" decision that didn't involve me but that reflected his own discernment that God was calling him to be Catholic. I wanted his decision to be about him.

I wish I had recognized then that decisions are more complicated than that. That should hopefully be clear now having read this book. I do think we have some kind of free choice—but not *absolutely* free, as though we could make the decision and no one else was affected or no one else affects us. For I am pretty sure it is impossible to make a "free" decision, as though we could cordon ourselves off into a space uninhabited by family, friends, church-goers, books, magazines, movies, and God. Once cordoned off, perhaps we imagine, we could make a decision that is true to ourselves, and once having made that decision, we rejoin society and announce to the world that henceforth, "this" will be our decree.

The gifts that the Holy Spirit gives are not gifts that enable us to be autonomous free individuals. Each of the gifts we have meditated on in this book involves relationships and communities, however imperfect, and all the problems those imperfect groups of people give us, in turn. The Holy Spirit's gifts are not ones that make decisions any easier or lives any more perfect than they were before.

Decisions are messy, and there can't be many messier situations than that of leaving one Christian communion for another. Jesus wanted unity but the unity we have is like a bungled-up UPS package, wrapping torn, half the box ripped apart, retaped, and the objects inside not quite in the pristine shape they were when it was first sent.

Paul's point to the Galatians was that if they accepted the gifts of the Holy Spirit, it meant they were going to have to find ways to live with each other, circumcised or uncircumcised, male or female, free or unfree. Paul was not going to give any of them the easy answer: "Form the perfect community *this* way, by excluding *those* people." No, rather, the gifts of love and joy and self-control and all the others meant that life would get decidedly more complex and involve, in some ways, more work. Paul knew that in his own life: he who had once been a keeper of the law and a persecutor of Christian communities was now doing the difficult work of rebuilding what he destroyed in his persecution (see Gal 2:18).

We *are* free, Paul says to the Galatians—but not free to construct a perfect world as we envision it individually, nor free to hope that any one decision we might make could make us into more perfect people. We are made free to follow Christ, made free to boast only in the cross of Christ, as Paul suggests at the end of his letter (Gal 6:12).

So, I am glad Joel became Catholic partly because of me: it was out of love and respect for me and out of a sense that our newly-made family by marriage ought to be unified if at all possible. But I am just as glad that it wasn't solely about me and that his decision wasn't as easy as simply "becoming what I was." His decision was also about the love of all his neighbors in Christ—his parents, his sisters, members of his former congregations—and that made it a difficult, messy decision.

Some might think that it looks like "I" won out. Joel became part of "my" tradition and some might even say that is as it should be, for marriages should be "equally yoked." But I do not think the story can be told that way. I didn't win; Joel's parents didn't win; and Joel, in particular, didn't win in this situation. Now it is he, like those Galatians, who has the unenviable position of negotiating how to live with all these different groups—circumcised, uncircumcised, man, woman. He is torn, just as the relationships between Christ's communities are torn.

Making this kind of decision is hell. Maybe there are times when it is easier to bear—maybe there are times when people are genuinely part of congregations that are so clearly abusive or evil that one knows the good decision. I highly suspect that is not the case for most "coming and going" decisions.

But I do think that if you are faced with this and you never make a decision, you never stand a chance of really receiving the Spirit's good gifts. You will always be in-between, always wondering like Paul's Galatians—circumcised? Uncircumcised? You will run frantically to and fro seeking escape and never see that the answer does not lie in either/or. I wonder sometimes if it was the frantic questions the Galatians asked that were the cause of the licentiousness and drunkenness and envy and all the other "acts of the sinful nature" Paul speaks of in his letter. The pain of wanting to be right, or at least of hoping the other side is not right, could well lead someone to want to "self-medicate" with the stupefying drug or sexual activity of choice.

Once you have chosen to stay or go, hoping of course that your choice was really about living in Christ as Paul prays, that is when the real work begins. How will you live now, with the people you have known and loved all your life? How will you love your neighbor as yourself? And will you allow others, even the others from congregations you are leaving, be neighbors to you? It is how you live after you have "made the decision" the shows that, indeed, this was not church shopping nor a search for a "perfect fit." Being willing to deal with, dive into, work on, or even embrace the messiness that ensues suggests that perhaps you have accepted the gifts the Spirit has to offer.

In January 2008, Joel and I baptized our two-month-old daughter, Lucia, in a Roman Catholic parish. She will be a cradle Catholic, though Joel and I were not. With us at the baptism were members of my childhood family and colleagues of ours—Methodists, Episcopalians, Presbyterians, Lutherans, agnostics, and seekers among them.

It was painful in many ways: to kneel when they were uncomfortable with kneeling; to pray prayers that were sometimes alien to them; to receive the body and blood of Jesus when they could not. And it was painful especially to see that even little Lucia is not "in communion" with members of her flesh-and-blood family.

The baptism was also a blessing and in it the Holy Spirit showed us some great gifts. Of course the Holy Spirit was there in some of the more obvious ways: Lucia received the Spirit at her baptism and she joins a host of people who have received the light of Christ and passed down the stories from generation to generation. Lucia has been made part of the Body of Christ, our Christian family—the family that ultimately supercedes any flesh-and-blood ties we have. As Christ said, "I have come to turn a man against his father, a daughter against her mother, a daughter-in-law against her mother-in-law" (Matt 10:35). Jesus does not exactly come across as a champion of the nuclear family.

And yet, the families Joel and I and Lucia have by blood ties are also family members in Christ, too. They, too, have been baptized and in any case, they are neighbors to love. One of the gifts of the Holy Spirit that day was to make visible how we are learning (despite all the messiness) to live in community with each other. We are learning to be brothers and sisters in Christ.

Thus, Lucia's grandmother and grandfather requested that we have the baptism, if at all possible, at a time when they could be there. They wanted to see Lucia become a Christian and they recognized the importance of the milestone even if they could not quite understand our family's newfound ties to the Roman Catholic Church. Her grandmother made the white baptismal garment that will be a family heirloom, though every once in a while she would shake her head and say, "I don't quite get why you want a white baptismal gown. We Methodists don't generally use the white garment." It is not easy for her, I know, to reconcile the fact that her daughter is no longer Methodist and will never be the Methodist pastor that was once hoped for. We prayed and ate cake and sang songs and blessed each other at this baptism. My family and friends demonstrated for me and to me some of the Holy Spirit's good gifts.

At occasions like this (and, between our families and friends and colleagues who are not Catholic, there are many) we continually strive to receive the gifts of love, joy, peace, patience, goodness, kindness, gentleness, faithfulness, and self-control that the Holy Spirit wants to give. The decisions Joel and I made, several years ago now, to leave the churches where we grew up and to join the Roman Catholic Church, were not the end. For once those decisions were made, the hard part began—not just for the two of us, but for all of us baptized—the world of the "new creation."

Bibliography

"65% of Women in U.S. have Eating Disorders." Women's Health News. http://www.news-medical.net/?id=37616.

Anscombe, Elizabeth. *Intention.* 2nd ed. Cambridge: Harvard University Press, 2000.

Ante-Nicene Fathers. Vol. 5, *Hippolytus, Cyprian, Caius, Novatian, Appendix.* Edited by Alexander Roberts, James Donaldson, and Arthur Cleveland Coxe. Grand Rapids, MI: Eerdmans, 1988.

Aristotle. *Nicomachean Ethics.* Translated by Terence Irwin. 2nd ed. Indianapolis: Hackett, 1999.

Armstrong, Donald. "Under Attack!!!" Sermon given February 17, 2008. http://www.graceandststephens.org.

Bonhoeffer, Dietrich. *The Cost of Discipleship.* Translated by R. H. Fuller. New York: Touchstone, 1995.

Brown, Toby. "Where from here? The narrow way considered." A Classical Presbyterian. July 11, 2008. http://classicalpresbyterian.blogspot.com/2008/07/where-from-here-narrow-way-considered.html.

Burtchaell, James T., CSC. *Collected Homilies Preached to Marianite Sisters of the Holy Cross.* Princeton, NJ, 1990–2000.

Buttrick, George. "A Simple Regimen of Prayer." In *Devotional Classics: Selected Readings for Individuals and Groups,* edited by Richard J. Foster and James Bryan Smith, 100–105. San Francisco: Harper Collins, 1993.

Byassee, Jason. "Going Catholic: Six Journeys to Rome." *Christian Century* 123, no. 17 (2006) 18–23.

Conant, Tom. "Thought for the Week July 13 2008." PastorTomVABeach's Weblog. http://pastortomvabeach.wordpress.com/2008/07/13/thought-for-the-week-july-13-2008.

Early Fathers from the Philokalia. 8th ed. Translated by E. Kadloubovsky and G. E. H. Palmer. London: Faber & Faber, 1981.

Edwards, Mark J., editor. *Galatians, Ephesians, Philippians.* Ancient Commentary on Christian Scripture: New Testament 8. Downers Grove, IL: InterVarsity, 1999.

Ferrara, Jennifer, and Patricia Sodano Ireland, editors. *The Catholic Mystique: Fourteen Women Find Fulfillment in the Catholic Church.* Huntington, IN: Our Sunday Visitor, 2004.

Harned, David Bailey. *Patience: How We Wait upon the World.* Cambridge, MA: Cowley, 1997.

Kosmin, Barry A., Egon Mayer, and Ariela Keysar. *American Religious Life Identification Survey 2001.* New York: The Graduate Center of the City University of New York, 2001.

Lewis, C. S. *Mere Christianity.* New York: Macmillan, 1972.

———. *Screwtape Letters.* New York: HarperOne, 2001.

Luther, Martin. "Praying in Faith." In *Devotional Classics: Selected Readings for Individuals and Groups,* edited by Richard J. Foster and James Bryan Smith, 132–37. San Francisco: HarperCollins, 1993.

Nelson, Gertrude Mueller. *To Dance with God: Family Ritual and Community Celebration.* New York: Paulist, 1986.

Nilus of Sinai. *Early Fathers from the Philokalia.* Translated by E. Kadloubovsky and G. E. H. Palmer. 8th ed. London: Faber and Faber, 1981.

Nussbaum, Melissa Musick. *I Will Lie Down This Night.* Chicago: Archdiocese of Chicago, Liturgy Training, 1995.

Perpetua, Vibia. *The Passion of Perpetua and Felicity.* Translated by W. H. Shewring. London, 1931. Medieval Internet Sourcebook. http://www.fordham.edu/halsall/source/perpetua.html.

Pew Forum on Religious Life. "U. S. Religious Landscape Survey." http://religions.pewforum.org/pdf/report-religious-landscape-study-chapter-2.pdf.

Radner, Ephraim. *The End of the Church: A Pneumatology of Christian Division in the West.* Grand Rapids: Eerdmans, 1998.

Radner, Ephraim, and Philip Turner. *The Fate of Communion: The Agony of Anglicanism and the Future of a Global Church.* Grand Rapids: Eerdmans, 2006.

Reno, R. R. *In the Ruins of the Church: Sustaining Faith in an Age of Diminished Christianity.* Grand Rapids: Eerdmans, 2002

———. "Out of the Ruins." *First Things* 150 (2005) 11–16.

Roetzel, Calvin J. *The World That Shaped the New Testament.* Atlanta: John Knox, 1985.

Rule of Augustine, The. Translated by Julian C. Resch and O. Praem. In *The Day of Pentecost: Constitutions and Appendices of the Order of Canons Regular of Prémontré.* 3rd ed. De Pere, WI: St. Norbert Abbey, 1998.

Rusch, William G. "A Survey of Ecumenical Reflection about Unity." In *The Ecumenical Future,* edited by Carl E. Braaten and Robert W. Jenson, 1–10. Grand Rapids: Eerdmans, 2004.

Schmemann, Alexander. *For the Life of the World: Sacraments and Orthodoxy.* New York: St. Vladimir's Seminary Press, 1973.

Scotland, Nigel. "Shopping for a Church: Consumerism and the Churches." In *Christ and Consumerism: Critical Analysis of the Spirit of the Age,* edited by Craig Bartholomew and Thorsten Moritz, 135–51. Carlisle, UK: Paternoster, 2000.

Southern, R. W. *Western Society and the Church in the Middle Ages.* New York: Penguin, 1970.

Teresa of Avila. *Interior Castles.* Translated by Kieran Kavanaugh, OCD, and Otilio Rodriguez, OCD. New York: Paulist, 1979.

Thomas Aquinas. *Summa contra Gentiles.* Book I: God. Translated by Anton Charles Pegis. Notre Dame: University of Notre Dame Press, 1991.

Vanstone, W. H. *The Stature of Waiting.* New York: Seabury, 1983.

Way of the Pilgrim, The. Translated by R. M. French. London: SPCK, 1963.

Wesley, John. "On Christian Perfection." In *John and Charles Wesley: Selected Prayers, Hymns, Journal Notes, Sermons, Letters and Treatises,* edited by Frank Whaling. New York: Paulist, 1981.

Westmoreland-White, Michael. "Encounters with Tradition (5): Becoming a Global Baptist." A guest-post on Faith and Theology: A Blog for Theological Scholarship and Contemporary Theological Reflection. http://faith-theology.blogspot.com/2007/06/encounters-with-tradition-5-becoming.html.

Yoder, John Howard. *The Politics of Jesus: Vicit Agnus Noster.* Rev. ed. Grand Rapids: Eerdmans, 1994.

www.ingramcontent.com/pod-product-compliance
Lightning Source LLC
Chambersburg PA
CBHW030844090426
42737CB00009B/1102